The Magical Power of Pendulum

Focusing Your Energy for Self-Improvement & Psychic Development

RICHARD WEBSTER

New Age Books

ISBN: 81-7822-254-x

First Indian Edition: Delhi, 2005

Reprinted from *Pendulum Magic for Beginners: Power to Achieve all Goals*, by arrangement with Llewellyn Publications, USA

Published by
NEW AGE BOOKS
A-44 Naraina Phase-I
New Delhi-110 028 (INDIA)
Email: nab@vsnl.in
Website: www.newagebooksindia.com

Printed in India
at Shri Jainendra Press
A-45 Naraina Phase-I, New Delhi-110 028

For two special friends in Hawaii,
Jon Kealoha and Laureen Tanaka

— Aloha —

Contents

Contents

Introduction

LIKE MOST SMALL children, I believed in magic. The world was an exciting place, full of unexplained mysteries. I believed in nature spirits, fairies, and giants, and knew I had the ability to communicate with them. I could talk to rocks and trees in the same way. I believed I could make myself invisible and perform all sorts of other feats of real magic. There were new and exciting things to discover every day. I never knew what might be behind the next corner. It was a special, magical time in my life.

Gradually, though, I learned that most people did not approve of, accept, or even believe in, the idea of magic. I was supposed to cast away my fanciful ideas and live in the real world. There was no such thing as real magic. It was a sad and disillusioning time.

However, despite the efforts of well-meaning people, the magic never totally disappeared. Every now and again, I'd experience or sense something that could not be explained away in rational terms. The magic was still there! Real magic. It was hiding, just as it had been before, but there were ways of releasing it. One of the best ways of doing this is to use the pendulum.

The pendulum is a simple device, consisting of a weight attached to a chain or thread. It is arguably the most underrated item in the magician's arsenal, as it can reveal information that could not be learned in any other manner. The pendulum reads energy patterns. It is able to extract information from deep inside our subconscious minds.

Consequently, it is hard to understand why it is not used more than it is, because miracles can be achieved when it is used properly. It is the perfect device to unlock the secrets of the subconscious mind. With the pendulum, information can be transferred from the subconscious to the conscious mind, easily and effortlessly. It can also work the other way. We can use the pendulum to deliberately implant information into our subconscious minds. The potential of the pendulum is almost limitless. Despite this, many people consider the pendulum a toy or plaything and fail to see the incredible magic that can be done with it when it is used properly.

The pendulum is deceptively simple. With just a few minutes of practice, anyone can use it. This simplicity is wonder-body as a pendulum that enables you to achieve the same results without carrying a pendulum around with you.

The pendulum is not a new invention. It has been used for thousands of years. In ancient China it was used to deter and chase away evil spirits, and to determine where they came from. The ancient Egyptians used a pendulum to determine the best places to grow their crops.[1] It is possible that the ancient Egyptian ankh symbol could indicate either a divining rod or a pendulum.[2] Marcellinus, the Roman writer who was active in the first century C.E., described a tripod that was intricately decorated with snakes and other animals that symbolized divination. From the center of the tripod a ring was suspended on a thread and answered questions. In Roman times, people were condemned to death for using the pendulum, probably because it was being used to plot against the emperor.

Ammianus Marcellinus (c. 325–391 C.E.) was one of the first people to describe the pendulum in detail. In his history of the Roman Empire he told the story of a group of people who were arrested for plotting to assassinate the emperor. One of the conspirators, in his confession, told of a priest holding a ring held by fine thread over a circular platter that contained the letters of the alphabet around the rim. The ring moved and indicated the letters T, H, E and O. This told the conspirators that the next emperor would be called Theodorus.

In 1326 Pope John the XXII issued a bull to ban the "use of a ring to obtain answers in the manner of the Devil." This shows that the pendulum was being used mainly for divination purposes in those times. The term for this is *cleidomancy.*

The scientific community took no interest in the pendulum until the end of the eighteenth century. Professor Gerboin at the School of Medicine at Strasbourg published the results of his findings in 1808. Abbé Fortis, Permanent Secretary of the National Institute of Italy became interested at about the same time, and also published the results of his findings.[3]

In the early part of the nineteenth century, Francesco Campetti, an Italian, began using the pendulum to find water and minerals underground. This attracted a great deal of interest and many theories were produced to explain the movements of the pendulum. Gradually, the pendulum began to be used for medical diagnosis, and this created a great deal of negative publicity. One reporter in Munich claimed that at the home of one researcher (Johann Ritter) the pendulum swung far into the night over "the delicate parts of nubile and naked females"!

By far the best-known name in the history of the pendulum is Michel-Eugène Chevreul. He became interested in the psychic world in 1830 while director of the Natural History Museum in Paris. He was fascinated with the pendulum and studied it for many years. Eventually, in 1834, he came to the conclusion that the movement of the pendulum was created by the unconscious will of the person using it. Chevreul found that when he stared at the pendulum he seemed to enter into an almost trancelike state. This made him conclude that "an intimate liaison established between the execution of certain movements and a mental act relating to it, even if the thought is not yet the intent to command the muscular organs."[4]

Abbé Alexis Mermet, a village priest, became known as the "king of dowsers" in the early twentieth century. This was only partly because of his incredible talent with the pendulum. He was also famous for his humility and willingness to help anyone, at any time. From his office near Geneva, Abbé Mermet successfully found water in Colombia, petroleum in Africa, and missing people and animals in a variety of countries. The Vatican used his talents to conduct archaeological explorations in Rome. Abbé Mermet's book *Principles and Practice of Radiesthesia* is a modern-day classic.[5]

In the early part of the twentieth century, the pendulum enjoyed a resurgence of popularity when it was marketed as a sex detector. In my collection of strange artifacts I have one of these dating from the 1920s. It is a pea-sized hollow ball of metal attached to a thread. The instructions were printed on a piece of paper the size of a postage stamp. These instructions say that the pendulum should be suspended over the palm of a pregnant woman. If the pendulum moves in a circular direction, the unborn child will be a girl. If the pendulum moves in a straight line, the child will be a boy.

Today, the pendulum is the most used item in the dowser's toolkit. However, as recently as 1930, the pendulum was considered an unusual device. In the October

1930 issue of *Psychic Research*, Harry Price reported on a series of tests conducted by Abbé Gabriel Lambert, a well-known French water diviner, in London. The Abbé used "a bobbin (rather like a fisherman's cork float, cone-shaped, and painted in stripes of bright colors) suspended from a thread in his right hand." In the tests, the Abbé was able to locate moving and still water underground with his pendulum. He also used it to determine the depth of the water, the volume and the direction it was flowing in.

The pendulum has been proven useful in times of war. The Germans used dowsers to follow the movements of British warships during the Second World War.[6] There are many accounts of soldiers in the Vietnam War using the pendulum to help locate hidden mines and underground tunnels. They were using the identical techniques that primitive shamans used thousands of years ago.

As you will shortly discover, there is almost no limit to what the pendulum can do. It can enhance your life in many different ways.

chapter one

Basic Stuff

THE PENDULUM IS a small weight suspended on a piece of thread, chain, or cord. Many people use a wedding ring hanging on a piece of thread. This is what my mother used. A paperclip attached to a piece of thread also works well. When giving talks on this subject to groups of people, I frequently hand out paperclips attached to a length of thread to allow everyone in the audience to experiment.

Commercially made pendulums are readily available at bookstores and New Age shops. They are available in every conceivable shape and size. I have a huge collection of pendulums, as my family frequently buy me ornamental type pendulums for birthdays and Christmases. They all work well.

I must admit, though, that my favorite pendulum is a commercially made one known as a Mermet pendulum. Abbé Mermet was a French priest who performed miracles with his pendulum. From Geneva, he was able to locate water in South America, and find missing people and animals anywhere in the world. He even helped with archaeological researches in Rome. The Vatican ultimately recognized him for his remarkable ability with the pendulum.

Choosing a Pendulum

The right pendulum for you is anything that looks attractive and is comfortable to hold and use. Ideally, the pendulum should weigh approximately three ounces and be roundish in shape, preferably moving down to a point at the bottom. When you start looking for a pendulum, you will be amazed at the variety of items that could be used in this way. A plumb bob from a hardware store works well. A button attached to a piece of thread makes a good pendulum. So does a piece of crystal attached to a chain. Lead crystal works well, but many people prefer quartz crystal because of the natural energies they provide. A crystal pendant that you can wear as jewelry makes a good choice, as you have it available for use at any time. Crystal pendulums are particularly good for healing work.

Some of the commercially made pendulums have a hollow compartment inside them. They are called "sample pendulums." The idea of these is to place a small sample of whatever it is you are searching for inside the compartment before starting to dowse. If you are searching for water, you can insert a few drops of water into this compartment. Insert oil if looking for oil, and gold when searching for gold. The Mermet pendulum has one of these compartments. The hollow compartment is not essential, but can be useful at times (see examples, Figure 1A below).

Almost anything will serve as a pendulum, but it is a good idea to have a special instrument that you use only for dowsing or magical work. At different times I have used car keys, jewelry and anything that could be suspended from a chain or thread. However, whenever possible, I prefer to use one of my special pendulums, because they are familiar, comfortable and easy to use.

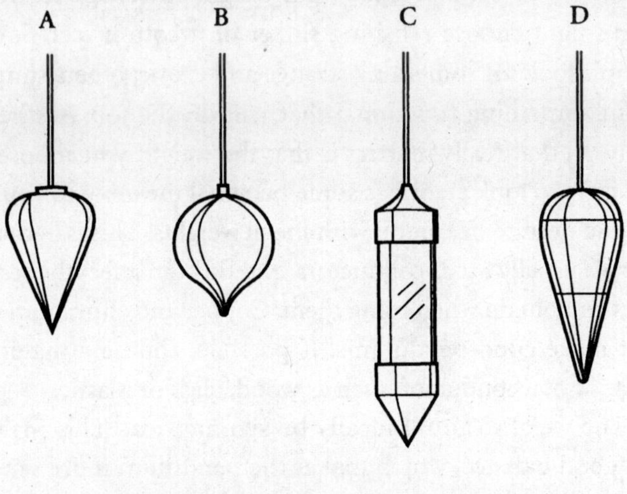

FIGURE 1A. Pendulum Types: A) Basic Drop; B) Mermet; C) Glass with hollow compartment; and D) Crystal

Whenever choosing a pendulum for myself, I hold it and ask: "Is this pendulum in harmony with me?" If I receive a positive response, I will buy it.

Making Your Own Pendulum

Many people prefer to work with a pendulum that they have made themselves. There is a lot to be said for this, as part of your energies naturally go into anything you design or make.

Take your time and choose the materials carefully. You might prefer a natural material, such as wood or crystal. One member of a dowsing society I belong to has a beautiful pendulum that she made out of a seashell. You might like to carve a pendulum out of lucite, or search for a small attractive object that is the right weight and shape for you. You might choose a fishing sinker or a cotton reel. Some people look for something strange and exotic; others simply want something functional that will do the job. Aesthetically, all that really matters is that the weight you choose is pleasing to look at, or has some personal meaning to you.

You need to be careful with metal weights. This is because metals usually act as conductors, and this can affect the readings you obtain when using them. Copper and aluminum do not make good pendulums. If possible, choose a material that is not a conductor, such as wood, glass or plastic.

The weight should ideally be symmetrical. This makes for good balance, which makes the pendulum more sensitive and easier to use. Round, spherical, and cylindrical shapes are the best.

Once you have chosen the weight, you need to choose something to suspend it from. Cotton or silk thread, string, cord, hair, and jewelry chains are the most commonly used items. I have also seen pendulums suspended from a leather thong, macramé, and braided plastic. Thread, string and cord have the advantage of being easily replaced when necessary. All that matters is that the weight hangs freely, and that the cord does not impede the movement of the pendulum. Attach the cord to your weight, and you are ready to start.

You might want to buy or make a small bag to keep your pendulum in. This makes it easier to carry around and there is less risk of the cord or chain becoming tangled. A pendulum that is protected in this way is also less likely to pick up negative energies. If you make your own pendulum, you might want to make a bag to carry it in as well. Alternatively, suitable bags are readily available at New Age stores in a variety of materials and colors.

How to Operate a Pendulum

It is usually best to start working with a pendulum on your own. Unless you have friends with similar aims and interests as you, you will find the presence of other people distracting when you first start. You will progress more quickly when you practice on your own. There will be plenty of time to demonstrate your new skill to others after you have used your pendulum for a few weeks, and become comfortable with it.

Most people prefer to use a pendulum using the same hand that they write with. Practice with both hands, but start your experiments with your right hand, if you are right-handed, and your left if you are left-handed.

If you are sitting down, rest your elbow on a table and hold the thread or chain of your pendulum between your thumb and first finger, using the least amount of pressure possible. Your elbow should be the only part of your body in direct contact with the table. Make sure that your stomach or other hand is not inadvertently touching the table. The palm of your hand should be facing downward, and the pendulum should be hanging about a foot in front of you. If you are standing, the best position is to have an angle of ninety degrees at the elbow, so that your forearm is parallel to the ground.

Make sure that your hands and legs are uncrossed. If you subconsciously protect yourself in this way, you will effectively close off the pendulum, and it will not work in the way it should. You can prove this for yourself once you have become used to the pendulum. Hold the pendulum in front of you and allow it to swing in the positive movement. While it is swinging, cross your legs or bring your feet together. You will find that the pendulum will stop moving.

Swing the pendulum gently back and forth to become familiar with the movement. Allow the pendulum to swing in different directions. Deliberately swing the pendulum in gentle circles. You might like to experiment with this while holding the thread at different lengths to see if the pendulum moves more readily for you when held at a particular position. Most people find the best length of thread is between four and five inches. Experiment, though, as you may find a shorter or longer length works better for you. A friend of mine has to stand to use his pendulum, because the cord attached to his pendulum is four feet long. (It is a good idea to tie a knot, or otherwise mark, the chain or string at the length that feels best for you.)

Once you have become used to the feel of the pendulum, stop the movements of the weight with your free hand. When the pendulum is still, ask it which movement indicates a positive, or "yes" response. It makes no difference if you think the question in your mind or say it aloud. Many people find that the pendulum will immediately respond and provide the answer. However, if you have never used a pendulum before, it might take time before it moves. Be patient. It will probably move only slightly at first, but if you keep on thinking "yes," it will start moving more and more strongly.

Ultimately, it makes no difference if your first experiment succeeds in five seconds, takes half an hour or even a week. Once you become used to using it, the answers will come almost as soon as you suspend your pendulum. Over the years, I have shown many people how to use a pendulum. When people have difficulty I find it helpful to have them stare at the weight and imagine it moving to and fro. For some reason, the pendulum almost always starts to move.

Another method that works well with people who find it hard to get started, is to have someone who is proficient with the pendulum gently rest a hand on the person's shoulder (the right shoulder when the person is holding the pendulum in his or her right hand). This simple action invariably causes the pendulum to start moving. If there is no one available to help you in this way put the pendulum down for a few minutes, and then try again.

In my experience, everyone is capable of using the pendulum. Consequently, there is no need to worry how much time it takes to get your pendulum moving. You do not need to be specially gifted or be the seventh son of a seventh son. The pendulum will start working more quickly in the hands of someone who is open, imaginative, and receptive to new ideas, than it will when held by someone who is logical, methodical, and precise. However, with practice, and a willingness to suspend disbelief, anyone can become proficient at using the pendulum.

Practice for five minutes at a time until the pendulum starts to respond. Once it has responded once, you will never have problems of that sort again.

Your pendulum will move in one of four ways: it may move backward and forward, from side to side, or swing in a circle, either clockwise or counterclockwise.

Make a note of the response that indicates a "yes" answer for you. Then ask what response indicates "no," "I don't know" and "I don't want to answer."

These responses will probably remain the same for the rest of your life. However, it pays to check them every now and again. I have known several people who have experienced changes in the responses of their pendulums. The best time to check the responses is whenever you have not used the pendulum for a while. If you are using it almost every day, the responses will stay the same. However, if you put it away for a month or two, you should confirm that the responses are the same, just in case they have changed.

Now you are ready to ask your pendulum any questions that can be answered with the four possible responses.

Start by asking questions that you already know the answers for. You might ask: "Am I male?" If you are, the pendulum should answer "yes." Obviously, the answer would be "no" if you are female. You can ask similar questions about your name, age, marital status, number of children, and so on.

The purpose of this is to get used to the movements of the pendulum, and to demonstrate the validity of the answers it provides. You will find that it makes no difference if you think the questions in your head or ask them out loud. The only times I ask questions aloud are when I am with a client and want them to follow what is going on. A friend of mine was embarrassed one day in a bookstore when he held his pendulum over a book and asked out loud if he should buy it. He suddenly realized that several people were also watching his pendulum to see what the answer would be.

Once the pendulum has confirmed the questions that you know the answers to, you can start to ask it questions that you would like to know the answers to. The pendulum is able to answer these because it can tap your subconscious mind for the answers, and then bring them back to your conscious mind. Your conscious mind knows a reasonable amount, but your powerful subconscious mind contains much, much more information. You could compare your mind to an iceberg. The conscious mind is the small part above water, and your subconscious is the much larger portion that is hidden from view.

Be careful with your questions initially. This is because it is possible to override the movements of the pendulum with your will. Let us assume, for example, that you are asking about the sex of an unborn baby. If you secretly hope that it will be a girl, the pendulum will reflect your innermost desires and tell you that the baby will be a girl, even if that is not the case.

Another example I remember is an acquaintance who asked his pendulum who was going to win the presidential election in 1996. He had been a lifelong Republican, and the pendulum gave him an answer that pleased him at the time. However, it ultimately proved to be wrong, as Bill Clinton was re-elected. The pendulum was responding to his deep, strong desire for a Republican victory.

Consequently, if you have an emotional involvement in the outcome, it is better to ask someone who has no interest in the outcome to hold the pendulum for you.

It is a simple matter to demonstrate how you can influence the movements of your pendulum using the power of your mind. Suspend your pendulum and hold it still with your free hand. When it is motionless, remove your hand, and ask the pendulum to move in a particular direction. You will find that after a few seconds the pendulum will move in the direction that you are thinking about. Now, think about a different direction, and you will find that the pendulum will follow your thoughts and move in the new direction.

Wishful thinking can also override the pendulum. If you ask: "Am I God's gift to women?" the pendulum may give an honest answer (which would be either "yes" or "no"). Alternatively, it might give you a mischievous answer ("I don't know" or "I don't want to answer"), or the answer that you secretly want it to give. Bear this in mind whenever you use the pendulum to answer questions.

The pendulum is not a plaything and should not be used to ask flippant questions. If you ask serious questions, you will invariably receive honest and correct answers. If you use it as a toy, you will receive the answers that you deserve.

The Coué Pendulum Test

Emile Coué was a French psychologist in the first part of the twentieth century. He became famous when he began encouraging people to use the affirmation: "Every day, in every way, I am getting better and better." These simple words helped many people, and when Coué visited New York thousands of people were waiting on the docks to welcome him.

He devised this simple test with the pendulum to demonstrate concentration.

You will need a circle, approximately six inches in diameter, divided into quarters by two lines that form a cross (see Figure 1B, following page).

Suspend the pendulum over the center of the cross and notice that the pendulum will move to follow one of the two lines. Watch it swing, and notice that the strength of the movement will increase.

Then, imagine the pendulum slowing down until it stops and then starting to move again, this time following the other straight line.

If you like, you can repeat this experiment with your eyes closed. You will find that this makes no difference to the result. When you open your eyes again, the pendulum will be moving in the direction you visualized. As well as being a test in concentration, this experiment also shows the power that you have over the pendulum. You can will it to move in any direction you wish. There is no need to help the move-

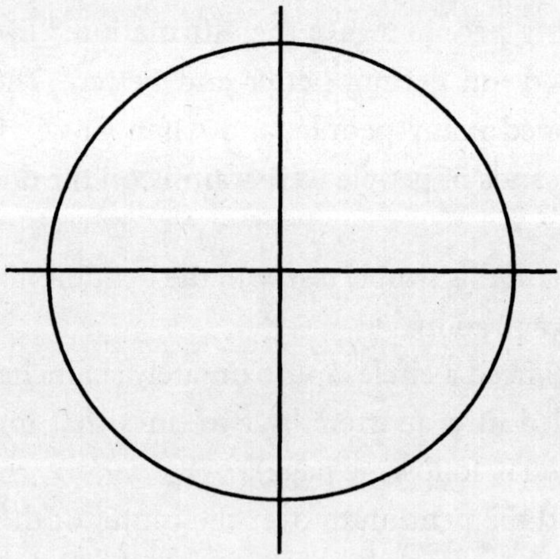

FIGURE 1B. Coué Test Pendulum Circle.

ment with your hand. Your mind is perfectly capable of doing it on its own.

Another experiment that gives the same result is to close your eyes while holding the pendulum. Mentally tell it to move in a clockwise direction. Wait fifteen seconds and open your eyes. You will find that the pendulum is moving in a clockwise direction. Stop the movement and close your eyes again. This time ask it to move in another direction, perhaps counterclockwise or swinging from side to side. Again, when you open your eyes, you will see that the pendulum has followed your silent command, even though consciously you did nothing to make the pendulum move.

How to Ask Questions

Many people have a tendency to ask questions that are impossible for the pendulum to answer with its limited range of responses. For example, the pendulum would not be able to respond to: "Should I spend my summer vacation in New Orleans or San Francisco?" In this instance, you should ask the question twice, once for each city. In fact, you could enlarge on the question by asking, "Would I have an enjoyable time if I went to New Orleans for my summer vacation?" Naturally, you would then have to ask the same question about San Francisco.

You may receive a positive response to both locations. If this happens, you could then ask, "Would I have a better time in New Orleans than I would have in San Francisco?"

No matter what the answer was, it would be a good idea to confirm the answer by asking the same question with the cities reversed to see what the response is.

Focus on your question while holding the pendulum. Repeat it over and over again in your mind. If any other thoughts come into your mind, dismiss them and return to your question. This is because the pendulum may answer one of your passing thoughts, rather than the important matter you are concentrating on.

Questions about work and career are common, and the pendulum can be extremely useful in determining the best path to follow. You can save time here by asking questions that include the words "instead of," "in preference to" or "rather than." Here is an example: "Should I return to college and complete my degree rather than carrying on with my current employment?" If the answer is positive, you will know what to do. If the answer is negative, you can reverse the question and ask it again: "Should I stay working at XYZ Corporation in preference to returning to college to complete my degree?"

Usually, it is best to ask a series of simple questions, rather than trying to formulate one complicated question that will answer everything with a single movement of the pendulum. In practice, you will receive a clearer answer this way, and the time difference involved will be negligible.

Sometimes you will receive the "I don't want to answer" message. When this happens, look at the way in which you asked the question. See if you can ask it again in a different form. You may find that you receive an answer by turning the original question into two or three simpler questions that ultimately answer your original question.

More Questions

You can use the pendulum in a number of different ways. Something I find fascinating is to ask the pendulum questions about my earliest childhood. My pendulum is able to tell me all sorts of things that I had long forgotten. By doing this I was able to discover what my first words were, how old I was when I took my first steps, and a variety of other information. If your parents are still alive you can ask them to confirm the pendulum's answers. It is fun to ask the pendulum questions of this sort, and your faith in the power of the pendulum will increase as soon as the answers you receive have been verified by others.

You can also ask your pendulum personal questions about yourself. "Am I afraid to reveal my innermost feelings?" "Am I a good person?" Naturally, you need to evaluate any answers that your pendulum gives to personal questions. As you know, your own needs and desires can overrule the movements of the pendulum. Consequently, you may get the answer you want to receive, rather than an honest response.

It can be interesting to ask the pendulum questions about other people in your life. Not long ago, distant relatives of mine had a vacation in our city. Before they came to visit, I asked the pendulum several questions about them, including their likes and dislikes. They were impressed when I was able to hand round cups of tea, already knowing who liked black tea and who preferred white.

Several months ago, a friend of mine was recuperating from an illness. He and I went away for a few days to give his family a break. Before leaving on the trip, I used my pendulum to discover what movie he would like to see while we were away, and what particular tourist attractions would most interest him.

If my wife and I want to go to a movie and have no idea which one we should see, I ask my pendulum. I usually suspend it over the advertisements in the daily paper, although I sometimes simply ask it questions about each film.

Experiments like these are not earth shattering, but they help to make life smoother and more interesting. The more you use the pendulum, the more uses you will find for it.

Asking Questions about the Future

There is no reason why you should not ask your pendulum questions about the future. However, if you ask questions about yourself, the pendulum is likely to give you the answers that you desire. These may, or may not, be correct.

For instance, you may want to know what the weather will be like on Thursday. Ask your pendulum if the day will be fine. Once you have determined this, you can ask further questions about the temperature, how cloudy or sunny the day will be, and so on.

Once you start using the pendulum, friends will want you to use it to predict the outcome of certain events, such as gambling. In my experience, the pendulum does not like to be asked questions of this nature, and will either decline to answer or else give you misleading or incorrect information.

Someone I know used the pendulum to try to pick the winners of horse races. It worked well initially, and he began placing larger and larger bets. Unfortunately for him, the pendulum began giving incorrect information and he lost the money that he had made. He finally realized what was going on, and stopped betting on horse races. In the end, he found himself in the exact same situation he had been in before starting to gamble.

When Should I Use the Pendulum?

There is no right or wrong time in which to use the pendulum. It is a tool that is ready for you to use whenever the need or desire arises. I usually carry a pendulum with me everywhere I go, but may not use it for weeks on end. Then I may consult it three times in a single day.

I know people who ask their pendulums questions about absolutely everything that is going on in their lives. These people must use their pendulums several times each day. I also know people who set aside time every week to ask their pendulums questions about the next seven days. I prefer to use my pendulum only when I feel the need.

Consequently, you can use your pendulum whenever you wish. Many people use their pendulums a great deal when they first become interested in the subject, and gradually use them less and less, until they are consulting them only on important matters that are going on in their lives. Others consult them all the time. It makes no difference how often you use your pendulum. It is a tool to be used, and you should use it whenever it feels right for you.

How Does It Work?

For at least two hundred years people have known that unconscious, involuntary movements of the hand holding the pendulum cause the pendulum to move. The subconscious mind of the person holding the pendulum causes the muscles to react unconsciously. This is known as an *ideomotor response* (*ideo* means "idea" and *motor* means "movement"). The pendulum amplifies responses that would otherwise be too small to be noticed. Consequently, the answers are coming from inside you.

Michel-Eugène Chevreul spent twenty years studying the pendulum, and one of his experiments proved this. He supported the arm on a block of wood at different places between the shoulder and the hand. He found that the movements of the pendulum decreased as the block of wood came closer to the hand. The movements of the pendulum stopped completely when the fingers that were holding the pendulum rested on the piece of wood.

However, Chevreul also noticed that he entered a different state of awareness while using the pendulum and came to the conclusion that there was a definite relationship between his thoughts and the movements of the pendulum. Chevreul's influence on the subject was such, that even today, some people call the pendulum "Chevreul's pendulum."

The pendulum gives us access to our subconscious minds. It could be said that it is an extension of our central nervous system. Consequently, it is not the pendulum that is providing you with information. The information is coming from your subconscious mind, and is being communicated through your nervous system. The pendulum is amplifying the messages from your nervous system.

A criticism that is sometimes made is that if we can influence the movements of the pendulum by using our minds, surely any information provided must be suspect. In fact, the opposite is the case. The pendulum enables us to tap into our subconscious minds whenever we wish. The subconscious mind can access the universal mind that knows the answers to everything. This is why we sometimes go to bed at night with a problem and wake up in the morning with the answer. While we were asleep, our subconscious mind asked the universal mind for the answer, and faithfully passed it on to us when we woke up. We do much the same thing when we are using a pendulum. The pendulum accesses our subconscious minds, which in turn taps into the universal mind, and the pendulum gives us the answer.

Consequently, we can ask the pendulum any question at all, and receive an answer from the universal mind. The best results occur when there is a genuine need for the answer. Your questions need not concern matters of life and death, but they should relate to matters that are important to you.

You can develop your skills with the pendulum by practicing experiments that may sometimes appear flippant or lighthearted. However, in practice, you are more likely to be successful in finding your lost car keys than in determining which of seven coins a friend touched. The pendulum will provide the answers to both questions, but will invariably perform better in answering serious, important questions.

Mastering the Pendulum

The pendulum is deceptively easy to use. However, you will need to practice with it as much as you can to become an expert. As with anything else, the more you practice, the more proficient you will get. You are bound to make mistakes when you first start using the pendulum, but these will become fewer as you progress.

You will move ahead more quickly if you follow a few rules:

> Never use the pendulum frivolously. If you can make the decision yourself, without using your pendulum, leave it in its bag.
>
> Do not ask the same question twice at the same session. This implies doubt. You must trust the answers your pendulum gives you.
>
> Never "show off" your abilities with the pendulum.
>
> Ask someone else to work the pendulum if you are emotionally involved in the outcome.
>
> Use the pendulum for good purposes only.

As well as this, do not let other people use your pendulum. Your pendulum becomes attuned to you, and you do not want other people's energies interfering with this. I have a selection of pendulums that I let other people use, but I also have several that I do not allow anyone else to touch. Keep your pendulum in its pouch or bag when you are not using it, and keep it close to you. This protects it and keeps it away from potentially harmful energies.

If you do this, you will progress quickly and smoothly. You will find that using the pendulum will make you more sensitive, aware, and intuitive in every area of your life. As this occurs, your skill with the pendulum will multiply.

The pendulum is a tool that can help you immensely. Use it wisely, and enjoy the many benefits it can provide.

chapter two

Honing Your Skills

EVERYTHING WORTHWHILE TAKES time to master, and the pendulum is no exception. Many experts say that it takes about a year to become an expert with the pendulum. Most people hate the thought of deliberately practicing anything, but fortunately, practicing with the pendulum is fun. Learning through play is one of the best ways to master anything. The experiments in this chapter are deliberately lighthearted, but will help you hone your skills.

In the early days of parapsychological research, scientists found that people usually achieved better results in the early part of each session, and that the success rates declined as the experiments continued.

They discovered that the volunteers tended to get bored after a while, and this is what led to the decline in the success rate. Consequently, it is better to practice for, say, twenty minutes on a regular basis, rather than for an hour or two every so often.

There are several experiments here. Practice each one two or three times and then move on to the next. There is no need to perfect the first one before moving on to the next. The idea is to have fun, and to keep your interest levels high. Approach these experiments seriously, but try them out in a lighthearted manner. You will achieve better results this way than you would if you approached them with grim determination.

Solo Experiments

These are experiments you can do entirely on your own. You will find that some of them will be easier than others. Interestingly, an experiment that you can do right away, might be a major challenge for someone else. We are all different, and what is simple for you, might be hard for someone else, and vice versa. Practice these in spare moments. Keep a record of your results. This enables you to monitor your progress and see how you are developing.

Lucky Card

Take five or six cards at random from a deck of playing cards. Mix them thoroughly. Look at the bottom card. This is going to be your "lucky card." Let's assume it is the Three of Diamonds. Mix the cards again, and then deal them out in a row in front of you.

Suspend your pendulum over each card in turn. Say, either to yourself, or out loud, "Is this the Three of Diamonds?"

The pendulum should respond in a positive manner over the Three of Diamonds, and give a negative response over the other cards.

Do not rush this test. Allow the pendulum enough time to make up its mind and give a strong positive or negative reaction.

A similar version of this test is to select several cards from a deck of playing cards. One card needs to be one color (for instance, red), while the others need to be the other color (black, in this example). Mix the cards thoroughly, and see if your pendulum can pick out the odd card.

Under the Cup

This test is similar to the first one. This time you need five identical cups and a small object that will fit into each cup. Let's assume that you are using a small ball.

Turn all the cups face downward on a tabletop. Close your eyes and mix the cups, so that you have no idea which cup is where. Pick up one of the cups, insert the small ball, and place it face down on the table again. Mix the cups thoroughly, so that you have no idea which cup the ball is under.

Open your eyes and suspend the pendulum over each cup in turn. Ask: "Is the ball under this cup?" The pendulum should give a negative response over each of the cups, except for the one concealing the ball.

It is important to do the first part with your eyes closed. Even though the cups are identical, you may be able to subliminally recognize the cup the ball was placed under by some small imperfection or marking. We see much more than we realize, and it would be a shame to destroy the validity of the experiment in this way.

Gin and Vodka

You need five identical glasses. Pour an equal amount of gin into four of them. In the fifth glass pour the same amount of vodka. Close your eyes and carefully mix the glasses until you have no idea which one contains the vodka. Open your eyes and suspend the pendulum over each of the glasses in turn. Ask: "Does this glass contain vodka?"

It is probably best to save this experiment until last, as you need to sample the liquid that your pendulum indicated to see if it was correct.

The Birthday Test

This is a test to see if your pendulum can tell you what day of the week your birthday happened to be on five years ago. (You can ask it to tell you the day of your next birthday, or most recent birthday, if you honestly have no idea of which day of the week it fell on.)

There are two ways of approaching this test. You might like to write down the days of the week on seven cards and suspend your pendulum over each of them in turn. Alternatively, you might prefer simply to ask: "Did my birthday fall on a Sunday five years ago?" Even if you get a positive response on the first day you enquire about, continue asking about the other days. This is simply to check that your pendulum knows exactly what it is supposed to do.

Once you have an answer, check to see if it is correct.

Double Blind Test

Select five or six small objects. You might choose a pen, a glass, a ruler, a paperclip, and an eraser. Write down the names of each of these on small pieces of paper, and place each one into an envelope. Line up the objects in a row in front of you.

Mix the envelopes thoroughly, and select one of them. Hold this envelope in the hand that is not holding the pendulum. Suspend your pendulum over each object in turn, asking: "Is this the object that is written in the envelope?" When your pendulum gives a positive response, open the envelope to check your accuracy.

You can take this experiment a step further. Instead of opening the envelope after receiving a positive response, place the envelope in front of the object selected. Take another envelope, and repeat the process, again placing the envelope in front of the object that was indicated. At the end, you should have all five envelopes placed in front of one of the objects. Open them up and check your results.

Experiments with a Partner

Choose a partner carefully. Particularly in the early stages, you do not need someone who is skeptical, antagonistic, or bored with the idea of testing his or her skills with the pendulum. Neither do you want someone who is simply helping you out. The person needs to have some interest in the subject. Ideally, you want someone who is as interested in the pendulum as you are. Take your time and choose this person carefully.

Take turns at holding the pendulum. It is better to alternate in this way, as it means both of you will remain interested in what is occurring.

It is important that you both remain entirely nonjudgmental. We all develop at different rates. One of you might be much more successful than the other in these experiments. However, twelve months from now, both of you should be equally as good. Keep encouraging your partner. You both need the other person to practice these experiments, and it is important that you both remain positive and enthusiastic.

To and Fro or Round and Round

Draw a large circle on a sheet of paper. Divide the circle into quarters with two straight lines. (You can also use Figure 1B, if you wish.) Ask your partner to think of the direction he or she would like your pendulum to move in. Suspend your pendulum over the middle of the circle, where the two lines cross each other and see what happens. There are four possibilities. The pendulum might follow one of the lines by moving away from and then toward you, in a to-and-fro manner. It might move from side to side along the other straight line. Alternatively, it will move in a circular manner, either clockwise or counterclockwise.

Naturally, it is important that you have an honest partner who will tell you if the movements of the pendulum were correct or not.

Sad or Happy

Ask your partner to hold out a hand, palm upwards. Suspend your pendulum over it. Have your partner close his or her eyes and picture a happy or sad event from the past. It is important that he or she gives no visible indication of what the scene might have been.

Ask your pendulum: "Is (your partner) thinking of a happy scene?" The pendulum will give a positive response if he or she was thinking of a happy event. No matter what the pendulum indicates, you will know if the scene your partner was remembering was happy or sad.

Tooti-Fruiti

Select several different fruits and place them in a straight line, a few inches apart. Turn your back, and ask your partner to select one of the fruits. Initially, have them pick it up for a moment, and then replace it. (Later on, after you have mastered this experiment, you can have them mentally select a fruit. In the beginning, it is better if they touch or hold the fruit.)

Suspend your pendulum over each fruit in turn, asking: "Is this the fruit that (your friend) held?"

The pendulum should give a positive response over the fruit that was selected.

You do not need fruit. Any group of objects will do. I frequently do this test with a handful of coins.

I Spy

Ask your partner to choose any object that he or she can see in the room that you are in. Suspend your pendulum and ask it questions until it gives a positive response. You might start by asking, "Is it the table?" "Is it the television?" "Is it the lamp?"

Another way of locating the object your partner is thinking about is to gradually pin it down. Start by asking if the object is in the half of the room that you are sitting in. If you get a positive response, choose an object in that half of the room and ask your pendulum if it is close to it. You might choose a bookcase, television, sofa, or chair for this. In this way, you will get closer and closer to the selected item, until you finally locate it.

Hide and Seek

Ask your partner to hide a small object somewhere in the house or apartment you are in. Write down the names of each room in the house on different cards.

Suspend your pendulum over each card in turn, asking the pendulum if the hidden object is in that particular room.

If you like, you can take this experiment a stage further. Once the pendulum has located the correct room, go to the room and ask further questions of the pendulum, so that you will be led to where the object is hidden.

There is another variation you might like to try, once you have been successful at it a number of times. Instead of having the names of the rooms face upward, mix the cards thoroughly, and deal them out name-side down. Hold the pendulum over each card in turn, asking: "Is the hidden object in this room?" You will be surprised to find that it makes no difference to the pendulum if the card is name-side up, or down.

You are Lying!

Mentally choose a number from one to ten. While you are holding your pendulum, your partner has to determine what number you chose. When your partner asks: "Did you choose number one?" you have to reply, "no," even if it was the number you selected. You have to reply "no" to every number. This means that you will be answering truthfully on nine occasions, and lying on one. By the time your partner has gone through all the numbers, he or she will know which number you chose. This is because the pendulum will tell the truth, even when you verbally lie.

You know that people can will the pendulum to move in a certain direction using the power of their minds. Even if you do this test with someone who is good at controlling the pendulum in this way, you will still be able to determine which number they chose. This is because the pendulum will change direction, even momentarily, before the person manages to control it with his or her mind. The pendulum is an extremely good lie detector.

Map Reading

You will need a large-scale map for this experiment. It does not matter what area the map covers. It might be a map of a city, a county, a country, or even the whole world. Ask your partner to mentally choose a place that is shown on the map. Suspend your pendulum over the map, and slowly move it around until it gives a positive response. Start with places that are well marked on the map. As you become better at this test, your partner will ultimately be able to choose anything that is shown on the map.

You might prefer to use a pen or pencil to indicate places on the map, while you suspend the pendulum from your other hand to one side of the map.

Card Sharp

You need a pack of cards for this experiment. Mix them up and then place them face-up on a table. Ask your partner to mentally select one of the cards.

Suspend your pendulum over each of the cards in turn. When you are over the card that was selected it will give a positive response. This experiment takes time to begin with. However, with practice, you'll find that you can move the pendulum quickly over the cards, and still easily determine when it is giving a positive response.

One Out of Fifty-Two

You will need a deck of cards. Remove the jokers and thoroughly mix the deck. Ask your partner to take a card at random.

Ask your pendulum if your partner chose a red card. If the answer is positive, you know that the card must be a heart or a diamond. If the answer is negative, the card will be a club or a spade. Ask your pendulum about one of these. Assuming the chosen card is a red card, ask, "Is it a diamond?" The answer to this will tell you if the card is a diamond or heart. Ask the pendulum if the chosen card is a court card (Jack, Queen, or King). If the answer is negative, the card must be one of the number cards. Ask about the numbers, one at a time until you receive a positive response.

Once you and your partner become good at this test, you can dispense with the cards altogether. Simply have your partner think of a card, and your pendulum will be able to determine which one it is, in exactly the same way as before.

Five Quarters

This test is one that my good friend Docc Hilford has become famous for. Everywhere he goes, people hide quarters under rugs and ask him to locate them.

Ask your partner to hide five quarters under a rug while you are out of the room. When you return, suspend your pendulum over the top left-hand corner of the rug and slowly move it around until the entire area of the rug has been covered. The pendulum should have given a positive response on five separate occasions. Once you have finished, lift up the rug and see how well you did.

A similar test can be done with drink coasters and a number of quarters. Have your partner place as many quarters as he or she wishes under a number of coasters. When you come back, hold your pendulum over each coaster, asking: "Is there a quarter under this coaster?" The pendulum will tell you which coasters conceal quarters, and which ones don't.

There are many other tests that you will be able to devise for yourself. They are a good form of practice. However, that is all they are intended for. The pendulum is much too important a device to be used solely for party tricks.

I must admit that on occasions I have been guilty of using it in this way. Years ago, I was at a party and divined someone's horoscope sign using my pendulum. This intrigued everyone, and I spent the rest of the evening working out everyone's horoscope sign. It was fun, but it was a rather frivolous use of the pendulum, and I felt guilty about it afterward. All the same, tests of this sort are fun to perform and will help you to develop your skills. Anything that helps you become an expert with the pendulum is worthwhile.

chapter three

The Pendulum in Everyday Life

YOUR PENDULUM WILL become a useful tool that you can use to help make your path through life as smooth as possible. We all make mistakes and errors of judgment. Your pendulum can help eliminate many of these before they occur.

Here is an example. After meeting someone for the first time, you can ask your pendulum questions about him or her. Is he honest? Is he loyal? Would he make a good friend? Should I buy something from this person?

You can evaluate anyone in this way. You should ask your pendulum questions about your children's teachers. Is this person a good teacher? Is he or she able to explain things in a way that my child will understand? Will my child benefit by having this person as his or her teacher?

You can use your pendulum to help you deal with anyone in your life. Not long ago, a woman told me how the pendulum had saved her marriage. She and her husband had been married for twenty years. Her husband had always been a heavy drinker, but over the last few years he seemed to be drinking more. She consulted her pendulum and asked it several questions about her husband's drinking habits. The answers were so alarming that she immediately sought professional help for her husband. He claimed that his drinking was under control, but reluctantly agreed to get help. As a result, he now rarely drinks alcohol and their marriage is better than ever.

You do not need to know the people you evaluate, either. Have you ever been on a blind date? You can use your pendulum to see how you will get along with the other person before agreeing to the arrangement. This can save time, and sometimes, many hours of agony.

A man I know works as the personnel manager for a large corporation. He uses a pendulum to determine important facts about job applicants before meeting them. This saves him a great deal of time, as he no longer needs to interview people who would not be suitable. He regularly uses the pendulum to determine important information relevant to the business.

Your pendulum can evaluate letters to determine the motives behind them. You can check signatures to find out the personalities of the writers. You can see if a check is good or not by suspending your pendulum over it. You can even determine if something is fake or genuine in the same way.

You can ask your pendulum questions about people you see on the television news. It is unlikely that you would have met all the candidates in a presidential election, for instance. However, you can ask your pendulum questions about all of them. Ask questions about their integrity. Will they keep their promises? Should you believe what they say? You may receive some surprising answers.

You may be thinking about introducing two people to each other. Your pendulum will be able to tell you if they will get along. This is a progression of a famous pendulum experiment known as the Two Coins Test.

Two Coins Test

You will need two coins of the same denomination. Two quarters are ideal. Place them on a table about four inches apart. Suspend your pendulum between the two coins. After a few moments, your pendulum will start to swing from side to side, going from one coin to the other. This shows that the two coins are in harmony with each other. Now replace one of the coins with another small object. A small packet of matches would be good for this. Again suspend your pendulum between the two items. This time the pendulum will not move from one to the other. Instead, it will either remain still or move backwards and forwards, keeping as far away from both items as possible.

Finally, replace the matchbox with the other quarter. Alternatively, replace the quarter with another matchbox. Suspend your pendulum and you will find that it swings freely from one item to the other.

Now you have seen how the pendulum reacts to two objects that are similar, and two items that are completely different. You can repeat this test using anything at all, even two people.

Suppose you are planning to introduce Vanessa to Michael. Neither of them is currently in a relationship, and you think they will get along well. Write their names down on two small scraps of paper, set them a few inches apart, and suspend your pendulum between them. In a few moments your pendulum will tell you whether or not to play matchmaker.

You can also use your pendulum to make a choice from a number of potential suitors. On more than one occasion I have been asked to help a woman choose between two, three, or four admirers. The procedure is the same as the Two Coins Test. I start by checking each person individually with my client. Often one or two people can be eliminated at this stage. If the pendulum tells me that my client is compatible with two of the admirers, I then ask the pendulum to determine which of the two people she is more compatible with in a long-term relationship. I ask as many questions as necessary, about different areas of life, and eventually the pendulum indicates which person would be the most suitable.

A year ago I did a similar thing for a man who had placed an advertisement for a partner in a daily newspaper. People could respond to his advertisement by leaving a recorded phone message. He received twelve of these, and was overwhelmed. His friends suggested he meet them all, but he did not want to do this.

Instead, he asked me to use my pendulum to determine which of the respondents he should contact. The pendulum gave a strong positive response to three, and he asked each of them out. I could have kept on asking questions until we got it down to one person, but it was better for him to meet a few people. He now has a permanent relationship, funnily enough with the person who accepted his advertisements at the newspaper office.

It makes you wonder why more people do not use a pendulum when you think about the incredible unhappiness and misery people suffer when they make the wrong choices in relationships. Everyone deserves a close, loving relationship and the pendulum can help in making the right decision.

A short time ago, my wife and I had a barbecue for about a dozen friends. Unfortunately, two of my friends do not get along well together. They are both intelligent, charming people, but have completely different outlooks on life. Every time they meet, they argue, and usually end up ruining the evening for everyone else. I wanted to invite both of them to the party, but consulted my pendulum first. I wrote their names down on pieces of card, suspended my pendulum, and asked if it would be okay to invite both of them to the barbecue. Much to my surprise, the pendulum swung easily from one to the other. I invited them both, and we had no problems at all. Everyone appeared to enjoy the evening, even the two friends I was concerned about. If I had not asked my pendulum for advice, I would not have invited one of my friends to the barbecue, and that might have caused problems later on.

I know several people who have used their pendulums in a similar way to organize seating arrangements at dinner parties.

Food and Drink

You can assess the quality of drinking water in different countries when you travel. When I was in India I used my pendulum all the time. On one occasion I was handed a glass of water. I checked it with my pendulum and found it to be perfect. My host then considerately added a few ice cubes. I checked the glass again and found that the water was no longer safe to drink. The water was fine but the ice was not.

You can use your pendulum to determine the nutritional benefits of food you are thinking of buying. If you know the brand name of the product you can do this from the comfort of your home.

An acquaintance of mine has a pendulum made from a wine bottle cork. He stuck a needle into the center of the cork and threaded some cotton into the eye of the needle. He uses this pendulum to decide which bottle of wine he will buy. He is convinced that his special pendulum leads him to the best wines because the cork recognizes good quality. I am sure he would experience the same results using any other pendulum, but he is not prepared to test any other pendulum. Besides, he has found that his homemade pendulum encourages people to talk to him, and he has made several friends because of it.

The Pendulum and Your Car

You are not limited to grocery items, either. Suppose you are buying a used car. You can ask your pendulum a series of questions about the vehicle before making an offer. Is the car in good condition mechanically? Does it burn oil? Is it expensive to run? Are the tires in good condition? Should I believe what the seller tells me? Is it a good buy?

You might be in a car lot and be undecided about which car to buy. Ask your pendulum. It might suggest you buy none of the cars. Alternatively, it will tell you which car would be the best one for you to buy. While you are at it, it would pay to use your pendulum to check out the salesperson, too.

The pendulum is useful once you own the car, as well. Nowadays, freeways can become jammed at any time of the day or night. Before going on a trip you can use your pendulum to decide on the best route to take.

Later on, your pendulum will be helpful in diagnosing any problems you have with your vehicle. It can save you a great deal of time and money when you know exactly where the problem is. In his book *The Pendulum and Possession,* Bill Finch describes how he adjusted his carburetor and located a bad plug using a pendulum.[1]

The same thing applies with household problems. You can determine what is wrong with a malfunctioning appliance before calling a repairman. A couple of years ago we had problems with our hot water system. My first thought was to call someone in to fix it. Fortunately, I decided to consult my pendulum first. Unknown to us, our infant granddaughter had somehow managed to turn the thermostat up to its maximum level. All I had to do was turn it down again. This example shows how impractical I am. However, over the years, thanks to my pendulum, I have been able to repair many things that would otherwise have needed professional attention.

Your pendulum can be used in a variety of ways in everyday life. I know a lady who uses her pendulum to help her decide what to wear. She regularly asks it questions, such as, "Should I wear pink today?"

Her pendulum is also useful when it comes to buying clothes. She can use it in a store to decide whether or not to buy a certain item. However, she uses it mainly with newspaper advertisements. When she sees an advertisement for clothes on sale, she immediately asks her pendulum if it is worth her while to visit the store and see what items have been reduced. If the pendulum gives a positive response she goes to the sale, and usually buys something. If the pendulum gives a negative response, she no longer bothers to go. She has learned from experience that the advice her pendulum provides is accurate.

Her pendulum is able to help her in other ways, as well. If she needs to buy something, such as a cosmetic or toiletry item, she asks her pendulum which store will have the item she needs at the best price. Her friends are constantly amazed that she always seems to know where to go to buy anything she needs at the best price. This is certainly making practical use of the pendulum in everyday life.

One of my students told me how she managed to find the ideal apartment using her pendulum. Megan and her boyfriend, Bill, had a German shepherd dog. Because of this, most landlords were not interested in having them as tenants. The couple also wanted a ground-floor apartment close to a park where they could walk and play with their dog.

After weeks of running around looking at unsuitable apartments, Megan decided to use her pendulum. She held the pendulum in one hand, and touched the advertisement with a finger of her other hand.

"Is this apartment suitable for Randy (their dog), Bill, and I?"

Megan would continue asking questions about each apartment only as long as the pendulum gave a positive response.

"Would we be happy living there?"

"Is there a park less than quarter of a mile away?"

"Is the apartment on the ground floor?"

"Does the landlord allow pets?"

"Will he rent it to us?"

By doing this, Megan and Bill eliminated many apartments they would previously have looked at. In fact, they looked at only two apartments. The landlord of the first one agreed to have them as tenants, but then his wife arrived. She did not like dogs, and the landlord reluctantly changed his mind. The second apartment they looked at was much better, anyway. It was larger, newer and more private. It was also slightly cheaper to rent. Megan and Bill lived there for two years until they were able to buy their own home.

These are all examples of how practical and useful the pendulum can be in everyday life. The pendulum is also extremely useful in finding lost and missing items. We will cover that in the next chapter.

Time and the Pendulum

The pendulum is remarkably accurate at determining time. If you are caught without your watch, an impromptu pendulum will tell you the exact hour and the minute. Ask the pendulum if it is one o'clock, two o'clock, and so on until you get a positive response. You can do the same thing with the minutes, if you need to know the exact time. Alternatively, you might be content to have the time to the nearest quarter of an hour.

If you have invited friends home for a meal, you can ask your pendulum what time they will arrive. This means that you will be prepared if they happen to arrive early, and will not be concerned if they turn up late.

Your pendulum can also advise you on time in the future. An astrologer friend of mine was trying to sell his house and buy another one. Unfortunately, although he found several houses that he would have liked to buy, he was receiving no offers on his existing home. He decided to ask his pendulum how long it would take to sell his house. The pendulum said twelve weeks. My friend stopped looking for a new home until three weeks before the date indicated by his pendulum. He received a good offer for his house a few weeks later. The time given by his pendulum was correct, virtually to the day.

Your pendulum can also pinpoint time in the past. A couple of years ago I was enjoying a few drinks with a friend, and he happened to mention that we had known each other for about four years. I thought it was longer than that, but neither of us could remember exactly. The following day I asked my pendulum about it, and learned that my friend and I had first met five years and two months ago. I immediately looked through my old diaries and was able to confirm the pendulum's accuracy.

Another useful thing to remember is that your pendulum can always locate north. If you are lost, or need to find due north for any reason, ask your pendulum to indicate north for you and it will swing in the correct direction.

chapter four

How to Find Lost Objects

HOW MANY TIMES have you, or someone in your family, mislaid the car keys? You know they must be in the house, but because you absentmindedly put them down somewhere when you arrived home, you have no idea where they might be. Normally this happens when you are in a hurry to go somewhere and cannot locate them. Everyone experiences this at some time or other. Fortunately, your pendulum will find the lost keys for you.

Thanks to my family, I have had an enormous amount of experience at locating lost objects with my pendulum. Whenever any of my three children lost something they would immediately ask me to find it with my pendulum. This was good practice for me, and I'm happy to say that the pendulum was successful virtually all of the time.

You already know that the pendulum can be used to receive information from your subconscious mind. Even if the mislaid object was put down when your mind was thinking about other things, the information will still be safely filed away in your subconscious mind. Your pendulum will be happy to release that information to you.

The most important part of the exercise is to remain calm and relaxed. It is difficult to use the pendulum when you are tense or flustered. Naturally, when something is mislaid we tend to panic and this raises our stress levels. You may need to take several slow, deep breaths before picking up your pendulum.

Here is the simple, step-by-step procedure:

Step One

Ask the pendulum a question that you already know the answer to. If you have lost your car keys, you might ask: Are the car keys in the house? You will ask this question only if you feel reasonably certain that the keys are indoors. Consequently, the chances are that the pendulum will give you a positive response. Occasionally, the response to this question will surprise you. You may have dropped the keys outside near the car. They may still be in the ignition. If this is the case, you will receive a negative answer to this question, and you can carry on from there. Knowing the missing keys are not inside the house will help you locate them sooner.

Step Two

Ask a question that will narrow the search down. You might ask: Are the keys in the living room? Ask questions about each room in the house until you receive a positive answer.

Step Three

Narrow down the search still further. If the pendulum gave a positive response to the master bedroom, you can do one of three things. You can visit the bedroom and physically look for the keys until you find them. Alternatively, you can ask the pendulum further questions to determine exactly where in the room the keys are hidden. Typical questions would be: Are the keys in the closet? Are they on the dressing table?, and so on.

You can take this as far as necessary. You could ask your pendulum about each particular drawer in a chest of drawers. Usually, though, before this stage is reached, you will have either found the keys or remembered where you left them.

The third method is to stand in the center of the room holding the pendulum and ask it to locate the missing keys. The pendulum will swing to indicate the direction in which the keys are hidden. Now, move to another part of the room and ask the pendulum the same question. Again, it will swing to indicate where the keys are. You will find the keys where these two imaginary lines intersect.

This method works well for objects that have been mislaid or temporarily lost. After all, your subconscious mind knows where the missing object is, and the pendulum enables you to retrieve that memory.

An alternative method can be used if you know roughly where the missing object is. In the case of the car keys, you know that they must be in the house somewhere. Hold the pendulum in your hand and slowly walk through the area where the missing item is. In the case of the car keys you would slowly walk through each room of the house. The pendulum will start to swing when you are close to the missing object, and will gradually lead you to it. This is more difficult than the first method. You need to be extremely sensitive to the movements of the pendulum. The sensation when you are getting close to the missing object feels like a gentle pull or tug.

Naturally, there will also be occasions when you'll want to use your pendulum to locate items that are totally lost. Neither you, nor anyone else, know where the missing item was left. Interestingly, you use the pendulum in exactly the same way that you did to locate a mislaid object. Instead of obtaining the information from your subconscious mind, the pendulum gains the necessary information from the universal mind that knows everything.

An interesting example of this occurred to acquaintances of mine recently. When their elderly aunt died, her lawyer produced a will that had been prepared decades earlier. However, a couple of years before she died, the woman had told several relatives that she had made a new will. No one knew where this will was, and a thorough search of her apartment provided no clues.

None of the relatives were overly concerned, as the woman's estate was small and the original will appeared fair to everyone. However, Martin, the woman's nephew had been experimenting with the pendulum and decided that this might be a good opportunity to test it.

Without telling anyone else, he asked the pendulum a series of questions. The first one was: "Did Aunt Betty make a new will in the three years before she died?" The pendulum answered affirmatively. Martin immediately asked: "Is Aunt Betty's most recent will in her apartment?"

The pendulum gave a negative response. Martin then asked a series of questions to try to determine where the will was. Her attorney did not have it. Neither was it in the house of any of her other relatives.

"Is the will in Pittsburgh?" Martin asked. This is where Aunt Betty, and most of the family, lived.

No, the pendulum replied.

"Is the will in Pennsylvania?"

No.

This was a major clue. Two years before her death, Aunt Betty and a close friend had enjoyed a vacation in Monterey, California. The pendulum confirmed that this was where the will could be found. It also confirmed that the will was stored in a legal office. Martin obtained a list of attorneys in Monterey, and asked the pendulum about each one. The pendulum finally indicated one lawyer. Martin called him, and much to his surprise, discovered that he had prepared Aunt Betty's final will.

The only major change in the will was a bequest to an animal shelter. The family were happy to do this, but still regard Martin's pendulum with suspicion.

This example shows that you can find anything that is lost, as long as you remain calm, patient, and ask the right questions.

How to Practice Finding Lost Objects

Finding lost objects is a useful skill, and you will find that your popularity with your immediate family will increase as soon as you demonstrate it.

You do not need to wait until something is lost before practicing this skill. Ask a friend to hide a small object somewhere in the house. Once this has been done, ask your pendulum questions that enable you to successfully find it.

You can also stand in the middle of a room and ask the pendulum to locate an object that you can see. Once the pendulum has done this, move somewhere else in the room and ask the same question. The pendulum will swing to indicate the object you are thinking about. This will give you faith to use the pendulum in the same way when something is actually missing.

Docc Hilford, a good friend of mine, is exceptionally good at finding lost and hidden objects. In *Dowsing for Beginners* I described how he successfully found coins that had been hidden under a large rug in a hotel lobby. Five quarters were hidden, but to everyone's surprise, Docc's pendulum uncovered seven![1] In this instance, he knew that the quarters were hidden somewhere under the rug. He walked over the rug with his pendulum. The pendulum responded each time it was suspended over a quarter.

With practice, you will be able to duplicate this experiment and perform real magic with your pendulum.

Finding People and Animals

With practice you will be able to use your pendulum to find anything you want. There are many recorded instances where a pendulum was used to locate missing people and animals.

Abbé Mermet was a humble priest, and in the first edition of his book *Principles and Practice of Radiesthesia,* he gave instructions on how to find missing people with a pendulum. Skeptical critics seized on the fact that he did not include any examples from his own experience. Consequently, in later editions of his book, Abbé Mermet included a number of examples, along with the comment that he could produce many more examples to anyone who remained skeptical.

Abbé Mermet required three things to conduct a pendulum search for a missing person:

1. A photograph of the person, or something he or she had touched or worn;
2. A plan that included the house or premises that the person left from, or alternatively, where they were last seen;
3. A map of the area.

One example of Abbé Mermet's talents was reported in the *Courier de Genève* in April 1935. An engineer had disappeared while travelling on business. His concerned family finally consulted Abbé Mermet to try to determine what had happened.

Abbé Mermet suspended his pendulum over the photograph and map and was able to deduce exactly what had occurred. While walking in the town of Valence the man had accidentally fallen into the river Rhône. The river had carried the body downstream as far as Aramon where it was lodged in a crevice. The relatives went to the location the Abbé had indicated and found the body.[2]

A number of people have specialized in tracing the bodies of drowning victims. John Clarke, of Leicestershire, became famous for this and located scores of bodies in the course of his career. Between March and May of 1933 he successfully located the bodies of six of these unfortunate people.[3]

A happier example concerned a missing twenty-six-year-old man who had disappeared from his home in Verdier. The distraught mother did not have a photograph, and gave Abbé Mermet a beret belonging to her son. Using his pendulum, the Abbé deduced that the young man had had a nervous breakdown and had gone to Toulouse. Twelve days later, Abbé Mermet received a letter from the grateful mother saying that her son had been found staying with friends in Toulouse. He had suffered a nervous breakdown, and the family were making arrangements for him to be brought home.[4]

In 1966 the Belgian police consulted Thomas Trench and asked him to use his pendulum to try to locate the body of someone who had been killed in the Brussels riots. The murderers had taken the body away with them. Thomas started with a map of Belgium. The pendulum gave a positive response close to Blankenberghe. Trench then used a large-scale map of the area and was able to pinpoint the position where the body would be found. When the police visited the site, they found the body less than fifty yards from the place he indicated.[5]

Abbé Mermet also used his pendulum to find animals. On one occasion he was asked to find a missing cow. The animal's owner drew a rough sketch of the site, and Abbé Mermet suspended his pendulum over it. The pendulum told him that the cow had fallen into a precipice one hundred meters deep, and was lying at the bottom, dead, with all four feet sticking up in the air. The man was puzzled, as he was not aware of the precipice. When he went to the site, he found the precipice, and the cow—with all four feet in the air.[6]

The person or animal does not need to be lost. Monsieur J. Treyve was a keen hunter who regularly used his pendulum and a map to determine where wild boars could be found. On one occasion, someone sent him two small stones and asked him to state where they came from. The only thing M. Treyve knew was that they had been picked up somewhere in France. It took him and his pendulum only a few minutes to locate the site.

He did this by asking his pendulum if the stones came from the north, south, east, west or center of France. The pendulum gave a positive response to center. M. Treyve then asked his pendulum about each of the departments in the center of the country. The pendulum responded affirmatively to Dordogne. M. Treyve knew that Eysies, an area in Dordogne, was popular with archaeologists, so he asked the pendulum if the stones were from this locality. Again, the answer was affirmative. He asked if the stones were from Eysies itself. The pendulum gave no answer, which told M. Treyve that he was close. He then asked the pendulum how many kilometers it was from the center of town where the stones were picked up. His pendulum gyrated three times, telling him it was three kilometers. He then asked if a man had picked the stones up. The pendulum gave a negative reply. He asked if the lady was pretty, and the answer was yes. The person testing him was amazed at the speed and accuracy of M. Treyve's reply.[7]

Map Dowsing

The potential of map dowsing appears to be unlimited. Verne Cameron, a professional dowser from California, proved that to the United States Navy in 1959. He contacted Vice Admiral Maurice E. Curtis and said that he could use his pendulum to locate all the submarines in the world's seas, and also determine to which nationality they belonged. The navy took him up on his offer, and Verne Cameron demonstrated his abilities to senior staff. It took just a few minutes to locate the American submarines, and he followed this up by locating all the Russian submarines. The navy was impressed but Verne Cameron did not realize how successful he had been until several years later when he applied for a passport. His request was refused because the CIA considered him a security risk.[8]

The map-dowsing procedure is the same for both animals and people. You will need a map of the area the missing person or animal was last seen in. Obtain the largest scale map you can for this. Start by asking your pendulum if the missing person or animal is still in the area shown on the map. If not, ask your pendulum questions about when the person or animal was last in the area, and in which direction they went. Then procure another map and start again.

You can hold the pendulum directly over the map, if you wish, and see if you can follow the path the missing person took. I prefer to hold a pencil in my free hand and use this as a pointer on the map. My other hand holds the pendulum to one side. I slowly move the pointer over the map. As I do this, the pendulum monitors my progress with positive and negative movements. This enables me to determine the route taken by the missing person or animal.

Whenever necessary, I pause to ask my pendulum questions. "Did so-and-so turn left at this intersection?" "Was he travelling on his own?" "Was he depressed?" In this way I gradually build up a picture of what happened.

There is an art to map dowsing. I have seen some people take to it naturally, but most people need practice to become good at it.

Fortunately, practicing map dowsing is an enjoyable exercise. Obtain a map of the area you live in. Start from your home and allow the pendulum to lead you to the home of a friend. You might prefer to let the pendulum guide you to a certain store, or a park, or school. This will show you just how accurate your pendulum is at map dowsing.

An acquaintance of mine used to travel to work every day on the freeway. However, he now travels by a different route that was pointed out to him by his pendulum. He had several different ways of getting to his office, and asked his pendulum to show him the quickest route. The pendulum chose a route that took him through quiet suburban streets. To his surprise, he discovered that this route was several minutes quicker than the freeway. He now enjoys the drive to work and suffers very little stress from his daily commute.

Once you have experimented in this way, you can proceed to more difficult tasks. A good test is to use your pendulum to locate a friend or family member. Start by asking your pendulum if they are in the area shown on the map. Once this has been confirmed, you can use the pendulum to pinpoint their exact location. If the other person has a cell phone, you can call them to check the accuracy of your pendulum.

I used to know someone who did her shopping in this way. She would ask her pendulum to locate anything she wanted that was slightly out of the ordinary. Her pendulum invariably reacted positively when she found a store or supplier of the item.

Map dowsing is a useful skill. Any amount of time you spend learning how to do it will be repaid many times over.

chapter five

The Pendulum and Your Health

NOTHING COULD BE more important than health, and the pendulum can be a useful weapon in the arsenal of all health practitioners. However, I believe that it should be used in conjunction with conventional medicine, and not be used on its own.

There are doctors in Europe who routinely use the pendulum as one of their tools for diagnosis. In France alone, more than 2,500 physicians use their pendulums on a daily basis.[1] Four French priests in the early twentieth century were the first to popularize the use of the pendulum for healing purposes. Abbé Mermet began giving medical diagnoses with it in 1906, and was quickly followed by

Abbé John Kunzle, Abbé Bouly, and Father Jurien. The techniques of Father Jurien became so popular that they concerned the medical establishment. They took him to court on six occasions, where he was charged with practicing medicine unlawfully.[2]

Abbé Mermet was more fortunate, and had few problems with the medical establishment. This might have been because he used his pendulum to cure the infant son of a doctor. The child appeared to be dying and was not responding to any treatment. With his pendulum, Abbé Mermet found that the problem was with the child's liver. Further questioning told him that the child could tolerate milk, but only if had been severely diluted with water. The child made a full recovery, and the doctor became converted to the power of the pendulum.[3]

Father Jurien enjoyed working with a crystal pendulum and conducted his tests by asking it a series of questions, such as: "Is there a problem with the patient's gallbladder?" or "Should the patient make an appointment with a specialist?"

Most practitioners operated in a different manner. The patient would lie down and the pendulum operator would scan the body. This would be done either with the pendulum directly, or using the hand that is not holding the pendulum. In both instances, the movements of the pendulum gave the operator the answer. This is because the pendulum would move in a certain way over a healthy part of the patient's body, but would change movement when held over an area that was unhealthy.

It is an easy matter to confirm this for yourself. Suspend your pendulum over your thigh. The pendulum will move to indicate that the tissue is healthy. (This will usually be the response that represents a positive answer for you.) Slap your thigh firmly and the movements of the pendulum will change to indicate that the tissue is damaged. If you keep holding the pendulum over your thigh the movements of the pendulum will gradually return to indicate a positive response, showing that the damaged tissue has fully recovered.

I first saw the pendulum being used for health purposes when I was about thirteen or fourteen. A friend of mine had several warts on one of his hands. He had tried all the usual remedies with no success. One day, an elderly man who came to tidy up the garden noticed the warts and volunteered to cure them. He used a button attached to a piece of thread as a pendulum, and we all watched as the button revolved around each of the warts.

"They'll be gone in seven days," the old man said confidently, and went back to his gardening. We thought the man was eccentric, but the warts disappeared within seven days, and never came back.

In this chapter you will learn how to use the pendulum to protect the health of you and your family.

Our health is to a great degree determined by our emotional and mental states. Long-term stress, for instance, ultimately affects our health. Tension reveals itself in tight, tensed muscles, particularly across our shoulders and in our necks. If we feel good mentally and emotionally, the chances are that we will feel good physically, as well. However, even in this situation, small health problems, such as colds, do occur.

Let's start with a simple example, such as a headache. Most of the time, you will know what caused the headache. You might have had an unusually stressful day and arrived home with a tension headache. In this case you will not need the pendulum to tell you the cause of the problem. However, if you suddenly develop a headache for no apparent reason, it is a good idea to ask your pendulum a few questions.

You might begin by asking the pendulum if the headache is simply a physical problem. Ask if a rest or good night's sleep will cure it. Should you take an aspirin? Ask the pendulum if you should see a doctor about it.

You can then search for the cause of the problem. Ask if it was caused by pressure or stress. Perhaps it was caused by something you ate. The pendulum will tell you. Maybe you are suffering from eyestrain. Ask your pendulum. If your headaches reoccur frequently you may need to make changes in your lifestyle. Again, the pendulum will provide the answers.

A friend of ours discovered she was allergic to chocolate by asking questions about her frequent headaches. She enjoys excellent health as long as she avoids chocolate. She can go months without it, but inevitably will develop a craving for it, and finally give in to temptation, knowing that the result will be a bad headache. Once she has recovered from the headache, she is free of the desire of chocolate for another few months, until it starts all over again.

Testing Food

There are many ways of testing food to see if it is good or bad for you. You can also determine if you are allergic to a specific food. I have already mentioned my friend who uses a pendulum to test for the presence of monosodium glutamate. She used to suspend the pendulum directly over the food to see if it was free of MSG. However, she felt embarrassed doing this in a restaurant. As a result, she now holds the pendulum in her right hand, below the table and out of sight, while pointing at the food with a finger of her free hand. Another commonly used method is to hold the food in one hand and the pendulum in the other. You can then ask the pendulum any questions you wish about the food.

You will find it interesting to test different foods. Place a wide selection of foods on a table. Include fresh fruit and vegetables, as well as chocolate and some convenience foods. Hold your pendulum over every sample and ask if the particular item of food is good or bad for you. You may get some surprising answers. You would expect the pendulum to tell you that chocolate is not good for you. However, if you do this test at a time when your blood sugar is low, you may get a positive response.

Sometimes you will be presented with several items that appear to be the same, but have been prepared by different manufacturers. You may, for instance, be in the supermarket and have several brands of butter to choose from. There is a simple test to determine which particular product is best for you.

Hold your free hand a couple of inches above the item you are testing. Suspend the pendulum over this hand and see if it gives a positive or negative response. Obviously, a positive response is an indication that the food is good for you. If you end up receiving two or more positive responses, you can test these ones again to find out which particular product is best for you.

Today, many people are concerned about genetically modified food. If you would rather avoid such foods, it is a simple matter to ask your pendulum if the food you are thinking of eating has been altered in this way.

The Well-Balanced Person

This is an experiment to determine the well-being of the physical, mental, emotional, and spiritual sides of your makeup. In Figure 5A, on the following page, you will find a circle divided into quarters to represent these four different aspects of your being.

Start by suspending your pendulum over the exact center of the circle and ask it if you are well balanced, physically, mentally, emotionally, and spiritually. If the answer is "yes," you have completed this experiment. In my experience, virtually no one is perfectly balanced in all four areas. Consequently, the answer is much more likely to be "no."

If this is the answer, hold your pendulum over each quadrant in turn, asking if you are well balanced in that particular area. The chances are that you'll already know the answers to some of these. If you are twenty pounds overweight, for instance, the pendulum is unlikely to give a positive response when suspended over the physical quadrant. However, you may receive some surprises.

Nicola, a young woman who came to me for a consultation, was halfway through a degree in anthropology, and was studying all the time. Yet the pendulum said that she was not well balanced mentally. We had to ask further questions to determine why. Nicola adored literary fiction and modern poetry. However, she was so busy studying anthropology that she had no free time to indulge herself in what she considered to be frivolous reading. The pendulum indicated that she would be happier, and more successful as a student, if she took some time out to read for pleasure.

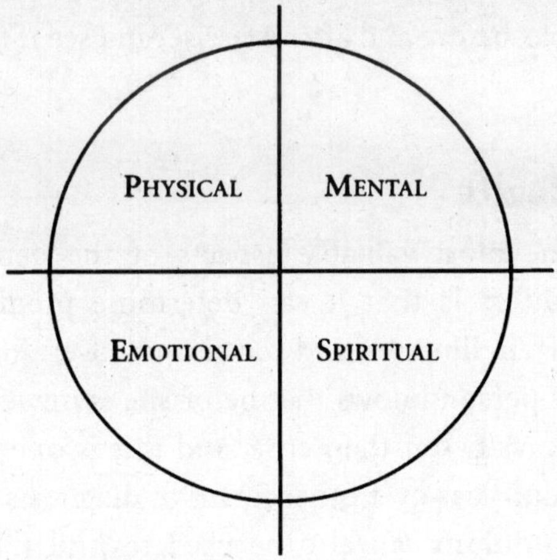

FIGURE 5A. Four Aspects of Being.

Of course, it is necessary to act on what the pendulum tells you. You may need to take up a sport, join a gym, or do some other form of exercise if the pendulum indicates that the physical quadrant is not well balanced. The pendulum will indicate the right form of exercise for you. You may need to read or study more if the mental quadrant is deficient. You may need to explore different faiths and areas of spirituality if that area receives a negative reading.

The emotional area is more difficult. You may need to ask a series of questions about this area of your life if the pendulum says that you are not well balanced here. Find out if the negative reading is caused by stress or overwork. Inquire about your relationships and other people in your life.

If you perform this exercise regularly, you will be able to monitor your progress. Try testing the physical quadrant, for example, before and after exercise, and see if the reading differs.

Good Health

One of the most valuable aspects of the pendulum in health matters is that it can determine predispositions toward certain illnesses, and can also uncover illnesses long before the person knows that he or she is unwell. Prevention is always better than cure, and this is one advantage the pendulum has over other forms of diagnosis.

The pendulum can also be used to find the primary causes of certain problems. Often the symptoms do not provide information as to where the illness began.

Healing Yourself

It is not easy to heal yourself using a pendulum because you are so intimately involved with the process. All sorts of subconscious fears and irrational thinking can prevent you from receiving an accurate diagnosis. In practice, I never try to ascertain my own physical health with a pendulum. However, on occasion, I have asked other people to do it for me. This is likely to be much more accurate as they have no emotional involvement in the outcome.

Homeopathy

If Dr. Samuel Hahnemann (1755–1843), the father of homeopathy, could return to earth today he would be amazed at how popular homeopathy has become. His method was designed to heal the whole body by stimulating the immune system. He did this by giving his patients remedies that in large doses would cause symptoms of disease, but in minute doses would cure. He called this the Law of Similars. This law says that a remedy will cure the patient if it can create the symptoms of the disease in a healthy person.

Dr. Hahnemann experimented on himself, members of his family, and anyone else who would volunteer. He had tested and proved ninety-one different substances by the time he died in 1843. Researchers carried on with his experiments, and in less than sixty years, more than six hundred remedies were available.

Homeopathy works on the physical, mental and emotional levels of the individual and believes that all levels must be in balance for the person to be healed. Naturally, if you are suffering from ongoing poor health it would pay to visit a homeopath, rather than trying to cure yourself by choosing from the bewildering array of homeopathic remedies available.

However, if the condition is not serious, you can use your pendulum to determine the best homeopathic remedy for you.

You can do this is two ways. You can visit a health store, with your pendulum, and suspend it over individual preparations. Alternatively, you can obtain a good basic book on homeopathy, look up the suggested treatment for your particular ailment, and then ask your pendulum if it would be beneficial for you. Another method is to use your pendulum over the complete list of remedies listed in *Materia Medica.* Once you have decided on the best remedy, you can ask your pendulum to tell you what the best daily dosage would be.

In fact, many homeopathic practitioners regularly use a pendulum to diagnose ailments, and then to ascertain the correct remedy.[4]

Bach Flower Remedies

Dr. Edward Bach (1886–1936) was a British doctor who became interested in homeopathy after realizing that certain personality types invariably suffered the same general patterns of ill health. As a doctor he was used to treating the physical body, but felt that the real causes of disease lay inside the heads of his patients. He came to the conclusion that illness was the result of stresses between the person's mental and physical states. He devised the Bach flower remedies to help restore emotional balance.

While vacationing in Wales in 1928, Dr. Bach gathered Impatiens and Mimulus flowers. In the same year he experimented with Clematis, and he administered these to his patients with immediate success.

Eventually, Dr. Bach discovered thirty-eight remedies. He wanted his findings to be used by the general public as well as the medical community. To help achieve this he produced a series of cheap booklets to educate and inform as many people as possible.

Because of their effectiveness in restoring emotional and psychological balance, particularly in times of great stress, the Bach flower remedies have increased in popularity over the years.

They work well with the pendulum. Whenever you are suffering from stress, strain, overwork, or intense pressure, use your pendulum to determine which of the thirty-eight Bach flowers would be most beneficial for you.

Edward Bach classified his flowers into seven categories:

1. Fear

Rock Rose *(Helianthemum nummularium)* This helps with panic, hysteria, fright, and unpleasant dreams.

Mimulus *(Mimulus guttatus)* For irrational fears, phobias, and timidity.

Cherry Plum *(Prunus cerasifera)* For bad temper, sudden mood swings, and fear of losing control.

Aspen *(Populus tremula)* For vague fears and apprehension.

Red Chestnut *(Aesculus carnea)* For excessive worry and excessive concern about others.

2. Uncertainty

Cerato *(Ceratostigma willmottianum)* For people who doubt their own abilities at making decisions.

Scleranthus *(Scleranthus annuus)* For indecision.

Gentian *(Gentianella amarella)* For people who are easily discouraged.

Gorse *(Carpinus betulus)* For feelings of hopelessness and despair.

Hornbeam *(Carpinus betulus)* For procrastination, and for fears that the burdens of life might be too great.

Wild Oat *(Bromus ramosus)* For people who are having difficulties in their work, or are dissatisfied with their current lifestyle.

3. Disinterest in Current Circumstances

Clematis *(Clematis vitalba)* For daydreaming and lack of interest in life.

Honeysuckle *(Lonicera caprifolium)* For people who spend too much time living in the past.

Wild Rose *(Rosa canina)* For people who are apathetic, listless, and resigned to their fate.

Olive *(Olea europaea)* For people who have depleted themselves mentally and physically.

White chestnut *(Aesculus hippocastanum)* To help overcome preoccupation with unwanted thoughts.

Mustard *(Sinapis arvensis)* To eliminate sudden feelings of melancholy and sadness.

Chestnut Bud *(Aesculus hippocastanum)* For people who keep on making the same mistakes.

4. Loneliness

Water Violet *(Hottonia palustris)* For people who prefer to keep to themselves.

Impatiens *(Impatiens glandulifera)* For people who are impatient, especially of others.

Heather *(Calluna vulgaris)* For people who constantly talk, but have little to say. They dislike being on their own.

5. Oversensitivity to Ideas

Agrimony *(Agrimonia eupatoria)* For people who bottle their feelings up and do not confide in others.

Centaury *(Centaurum umbellatum)* For people who find it hard to turn down the requests of others.

Walnut *(Juglans regia)* For people who need help in balancing their emotions during periods of change.

Holly *(Ilex aquifolium)* To eliminate feelings of envy, jealousy, suspicion, and hatred.

6. Despondency and Despair

Larch *(Larix decidua)* For lack of confidence.

Pine *(Pinus sylvestris)* For people who constantly blame themselves for everything that is going on around them.

Elm *(Ulmus procera)* For people who feel overwhelmed.

Sweet Chestnut *(Castanea sativa)* To help overcome feelings of despair.

Star of Bethlehem *(Ornithogalum umbellatum)* For severe mental and emotional stress.

Willow *(Salix vitellina)* To help eliminate feelings of bitterness and resentment.

Oak *(Quercus robur)* To help people overcome their limitations and achieve success.

Crab Apple *(Malus pumila)* For people with low self-esteem and a poor self image.

7. Overly concerned about Others' Welfare

Chicory *(Cichorium intybus)* For people who are overly possessive and demanding.

Vervain *(Verbena officinalis)* For people who are domineering and feel that their views are more important than those of others.

Vine *(Vitis Vinifera)* For people who are domineering, ruthless and obstinate.

Beech *(Fagus sylvatica)* For people who constantly find fault in others.

Rock water *(Aqua petra)* For people who are overly hard on themselves.

You can use your pendulum to determine which flower remedies you need.[5] The pendulum will also advise you as to the correct amount required. It is possible to prepare your own Bach flower remedies, but they are available from natural health practitioners at modest prices. Rather than make my own, I buy Bach flower remedies as and when required.

The Chakras

We are much more than a physical body. Healing involves the mind, body and spirit of the person being treated. Consequently, it is important to heal our mental, emotional and spiritual bodies, as well as the physical one.

Our physical body is surrounded by an invisible energy field known as the aura. I believe, that with practice, anyone can learn to see auras.[6]

Inside the aura are seven energy centers, known as chakras (see Figure 5B on the following page). They are situated along the length of the spine, and are revolving, funnel-like circles of subtle energy. They absorb higher energies and transform them into a form that can be used by

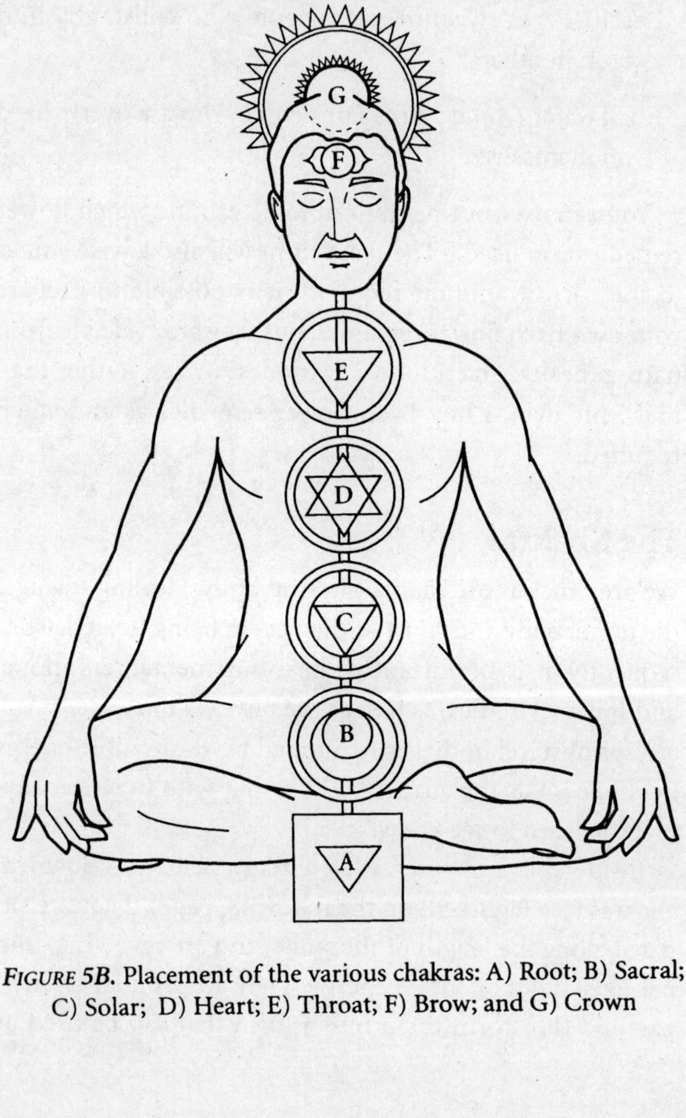

FIGURE 5B. Placement of the various chakras: A) Root; B) Sacral; C) Solar; D) Heart; E) Throat; F) Brow; and G) Crown

the physical body. The word *chakra* comes from the Sanskrit and means "wheel." This is a good name for them as the chakras are constantly rotating. This rotation allows the chakras to attract and give off energy.

The chakras relate to the physical systems of excretion, reproduction, digestion, circulation, respiration, and the central nervous system.

However, they also relate to our emotional and spiritual systems. Our emotions can be read in the chakras on a daily basis. Our approach and attitude toward life are revealed clearly in the state of our chakras. If our personal philosophy and approach to life change, this will be clearly revealed in the chakras.

For instance, many people have root and solar chakras that are noticeably more developed than the others. These people are materialistic and give no attention to spiritual or philosophical matters. A more spiritually minded person will have chakras that are better balanced, and will be using the top three chakras to the same extent as the bottom four.

The Quatern

The lower four chakras create what is known as the quatern. They have a lower vibration than the top three chakras and are related to the elements of fire, earth, air, and water.

The Root Chakra

The root chakra is situated at the base of the spine and is related to feelings of security and comfort. It transfers universal energies into the physical level, and allows these to filter into our subtle system. The root chakra keeps us firmly grounded to the earth. In fact, it is related to the earth element. It is red, and is often depicted as a four-petalled lotus. In the physical body it is related to the anus, rectum, colon, and prostate gland. It also is associated with the spinal column.

The Sacral Chakra

The sacral chakra is situated at the level of the sacrum in the small of the back, about two inches from the navel. It is related to the water element and is concerned with the fluidic aspects of the body. It cleanses and purifies the subtle body. The sacral chakra relates to creative, emotional balance, and sexual expression. The sacral chakra is orange, and is depicted as a six-petaled lotus. In the physical body it is related to the reproductive system.

The Solar Chakra

The solar chakra is situated at the level of the solar plexus. It is related to the fire element, and possesses the positive aspects of fire, such as warmth, light, energy, and purification. The solar chakra is concerned with warmth, happiness, and self-esteem. Emotional energy comes from this chakra. It is yellow in color and is depicted as a ten-petaled lotus. In the physical body it is related to the digestive system and the lower back.

The Heart Chakra

The heart chakra is situated in line with the heart, in the center of the chest. It is related to the air element, and is concerned with understanding, devotion, love, and the sense of touch. Empathy and sympathy come from this chakra. The heart chakra is green in color, and is depicted as a twelve-petaled lotus. In the physical body it is related to the heart, lungs, and upper back.

The Trinity

The three top chakras are known as the trinity, or the triad. They are related to the three quadruplicities of astrology, known as cardinal, fixed, and mutable. The cardinal signs (Aries, Cancer, Libra, and Capricorn) are outgoing and expressive. The fixed signs (Taurus, Leo, Scorpio, and Aquarius) are stubborn and tenacious. The mutable signs (Gemini, Virgo, Sagittarius, and Pisces) and adaptable and can change quickly to suit different conditions.

The Throat Chakra

The throat chakra is situated at the level of the throat. It plays a vital role in transmitting information from the brow chakra to the lower ones. Consequently, it connects our thoughts and feelings. It relates to communication, self-expression, sound, and the voice. The throat chakra is blue and is depicted as a sixteen-petaled lotus. In the physical body it is related to respiration, the neck, ears, and arms.

The Brow Chakra

The brow chakra is situated in the forehead, between the eyebrows. It governs the mind, thought, and intuition. It is sometimes referred to as "the third eye." It is indigo in color and is depicted as a ninety-six-petaled lotus. In the physical body it is related to the thinking processes. It is also concerned with the sinuses.

The Crown Chakra

The crown chakra is situated at the top of the head. It balances and harmonizes all sides of our nature. The crown chakra gathers together and unites all the energies of the other six chakras. It gives us access to the infinite. The crown chakra is violet, and is depicted as a thousand-petaled lotus.

Malfunctions can occur with each chakra. Here are some of the possible physical side effects that can occur when the chakras are not working as they should:

> *Root chakra:* hemorrhoids, constipation, and prostate problems.
>
> *Sacral chakra:* impotence, frigidity, menstrual problems, problems with the kidneys or gallbladder.
>
> *Solar chakra:* eating disorders, ulcers.
>
> *Heart chakra:* angina, hypertension.
>
> *Throat chakra:* sore throats, problems with the voice.
>
> *Brow chakra:* headaches, fuzzy or illogical thinking.
>
> *Crown chakra:* loneliness, isolation, inability to see other people's points of view.

You can use your pendulum to determine the well-being of each individual chakra.

Aura Balancing

Aura balancing is a simple process that literally has the power to change lives. We hold emotional blockages of all sorts inside the chakras. Once they are released in this process, the person feels, and often looks, ten years younger.

Ask your client to lie on his or her back. Suspend your pendulum over the base of the spine (the genital area), and ask your pendulum: "Is my friend's root chakra in good health?" The pendulum will give a positive or negative reply. If the answer is positive, nothing further needs to be done with the root chakra and you can move on to ask the same question about the sacral chakra.

However, if you receive a negative response to this question about the root chakra further action is required. In practice, I check all of the chakras before starting to work on the chakras that are out of balance.

Once you have checked all the chakras, determine which chakra is the most negative. You do this by asking the following question about each chakra in turn: "Is the root chakra the most negative?" "Is the sacral chakra the most negative?" Before proceeding further, you need to ask your pendulum two further questions: "Which movement indicates negative energies?" and "Which movement indicates positive energies?"

Fill a glass of water and place the fingers of the hand that is not using the pendulum into it. Suspend it over the chakra that is most negative and ask the pendulum to remove all the negative energies from it. It will start moving in the direction that indicates negative energies. This shows that the pendulum is extracting the negative energies, and that they are coming up the pendulum, into your arm, across your chest, and down into the glass of water.

When the pendulum stops moving in the negative direction, take your fingers out of the water and wash your hands thoroughly under running water.

Repeat the process with the next most negative chakra, and continue until all the negative chakras have been treated in this way.

When you have treated all of the negative chakras, go through all seven chakras again to ensure that you get a positive reading from each one. Sometimes you will find that not all of the negativity has been removed, and the process needs to be repeated. The aura balancing is not finished until you receive a positive reading from each chakra.

I like to discuss what is going on with each client while working with them. Some clients like to talk about their problems, while others don't. Some people are reluctant to discuss emotional issues. If this is the case, I still explain what I am doing, and why I am doing it, but talk about it in more general terms than I would otherwise.

Here are some of the emotional factors that can cause blockages in the chakras:

Root chakra: insecurity, self-doubt, unwillingness to let go of the past.

Sacral chakra: selfishness, self-centeredness, inability to communicate well with others.

Solar chakra: low self-esteem, feelings of powerlessness.

Heart chakra: inability to express emotions, holding back, lack of empathy.

Throat chakra: Lack of verbal skills creating feelings of frustration. Inability to express innermost feelings.

Brow chakra: Living in a dream world, fantasies.

Crown chakra: Feelings of isolation and alienation from others. Rigid, stubborn outlook.

Obviously, it is impossible to use the pendulum in this way to check your own chakras. However, you can check on their well-being by asking your pendulum questions about each chakra. It is possible to repair blocked chakras in the same way, but it is better to find someone else to this for you. However, if necessary, it can be done.

Crystals and the Chakras

There are crystals that relate to each of the chakras. Many people find benefit from wearing or carrying a crystal that relates to a specific chakra. However this needs to be done with care as crystals are quick to pick up energy, both positive and negative. If you spend most of your time with negative people, any crystals you are wearing will quickly absorb that negative energy and feed it back to you. On the other hand, if you spend most of your time with enthusiastic and positive people, your crystals will absorb that and allow you to reap the benefits.

Crystals should be worn as close to the skin as possible. If you have them under your clothing, they will be less likely to absorb negative energies from others.

You should cleanse your crystals frequently by rinsing them in cold running water for sixty seconds. The termination point of the crystal should be held downwards when you do this.

The crystals for each chakra are chosen by color. Consequently, a red crystal helps to stimulate the root chakra. Clear quartz crystals are also good. They relate to light, which creates all the colors, and can help stimulate healing in any, and all, of the chakras.

Here are suggested crystals for each chakra:

Root chakra: red garnet (should be worn below the waist as it can cause dizziness and headaches), black obsidian (helps to ground the person), smoky quartz (helps remove blockages of all types).

Sacral chakra: tiger's eye (provides strength, courage and endurance), carnelian (reduces tension and increases virility).

Solar chakra: citrine (good for concentration), malachite (releases emotional trauma and creates feelings of well-being)

Heart chakra: green jade (for love and wisdom), rose quartz (good for nurturing the self), green aventurine (known as the "dreamer's stone" as it encourages great ideas and independence).

Throat chakra: sodalite (helps self-expression), azurite (for spiritual growth),

Brow chakra: lapis (aids spirituality), fluorite (good to wear after emotional upsets).

Crown chakra: amethyst (for protection), purple fluorite (restores body and soul), sugilite (helps provide a sense of purpose), clear quartz (provides the entire rainbow and aids all the chakras).

You can use your pendulum to help you find the right gemstone for you. You can start by asking your pendulum about different types of crystals and gemstones. It might, for example, suggest that you would benefit by wearing green aventurine. Once you have determined that, suspend your pendulum over several specimens of aventurine to determine the one that is best for you.

Healing Others

You can use your pendulum to help heal others in a number of ways. Obviously, you must start by diagnosing the problem. You can use Father Jurien's method of going through the body asking the pendulum about every organ in a step-by-step manner. Alternatively, you can scan the body with the pendulum while watching the movements of the pendulum for any irregularities. Start by asking the pendulum to indicate the correct movements to indicate a healthy organ, and an unhealthy one.

You may uncover old injuries while doing this. Many years ago, I was scanning a friend for health, and my pendulum indicated a problem in her right knee. She was insistent that there was nothing wrong with her knee. While driving home, she realized what my pendulum had picked up. She had damaged her right knee while playing tennis twelve months earlier. She thought her knee had fully recovered, but my pendulum indicated that it had not completely repaired itself yet. This has occurred on several occasions since. Obviously, the pendulum is sensitive enough to pick up health factors that the patient is not consciously aware of.

Obviously, if your pendulum uncovers a major illness, you should send the patient to a medical doctor for further diagnosis and treatment.

Once you have located the area of "dis-ease," you can use the pendulum to determine the best cause of treatment. This might be homeopathy, naturopathy, Bach flowers, herbs, acupuncture, conventional medicine, exercise, a change in diet, or some other method of treatment. Ask your pendulum to determine the best course of action.

You can also use your pendulum to determine the efficiency of any remedies you are using. Hold the pendulum over the remedy and ask if the patient will be helped by taking this particular remedy. If the same remedy is available from a number of manufacturers you can determine which brand would be the most beneficial for the patient.

Absent Healing

You can use your pendulum to send absent healing to others. It makes no difference where in the world they may be. I like to have permission from the person I am sending healing to.

Surprising as it may seem, many people do not want to get well. They enjoy the extra attention they receive from others, and consequently, would not be thankful for any healing you sent them. Of course, there will be occasions when you cannot receive permission. The person may be unconscious, or you may not know how to contact them.

I prefer to do this ritual in the evening with the business of the day behind me. You will need two white candles to represent you and the person you are sending healing to. Light the candles and place them in front of you, about a foot apart. Take several deep breaths and then allow the pendulum to swing in an arc from one candle to the other. Visualize healing being carried from the candle on your left (representing you) to the candle on your right (the person needing healing).

Do this for as long as feels comfortable for you. Stop as soon as you find your mind becoming distracted with other thoughts.

Stop the swinging of the pendulum with your free hand, blow out the candle that represents you (left), and then the candle that represents the person receiving healing.

Before getting up, think about the person you have just sent healing to. Picture him or her fully restored to health and vigor. See this in your imagination as clearly as you can, and then let the picture go. Carry on with your evening, confident that you have done something valuable for your friend.

You can use the same technique to send love to someone else. Again use two white candles, to represent the two of you, and send thoughts of love through the pendulum to the other person.

This technique is extremely valuable for close relationships. It can bring the two of you closer than ever. Naturally, most people assume that this exercise should be done between two people who are in, or at least have the potential to be in, a close, loving romantic relationship. However, there are benefits in sending love to everyone you know. It can also be used to heal rifts between two people. It is an incredible exercise to send love to someone who hates you. I have seen instances where hate has turned into close friendship, thanks to this ritual.

Absent Scanning

You can use your pendulum to determine the health of people anywhere in the world. Start by asking if the person is in good health. Then ask about each chakra. If you locate any areas of discomfort or "dis-ease," you can send remote healing to that person.

Animal Health

The pendulum is extremely useful when a pet, or other animal, is ill. Naturally, the animal will not be able to tell you what the problem is, but your pendulum will provide the answer, if you ask it the right questions.

It is best to have a standard procedure for doing this. Years ago, I met a man who made his living by dowsing the health of horses. He would stand by the horse's head with his pendulum in his hand. He held his other hand palm upward to receive universal energies. He also closed his eyes during parts of his evaluation. The rest of the time he would gaze into the horse's eyes. He rarely looked at what his pendulum was doing.

He always began by asking the pendulum questions about the horse's diet. These were specific questions, relating to different minerals and elements that should be present in the horse's food.

He then asked questions about the horse's internal organs. He seemed to go into a trance while evaluating these with his pendulum. He spoke quickly and softly, while his wife wrote down his findings.

He then asked if the horse was uncomfortable, or in pain. He paid special attention to the horse's shoulders, legs, and hooves.

He asked the pendulum if the saddle and reins were comfortable, and finished by asking the horse if it had anything to add.

The entire process took about thirty minutes. This man did not claim to be a healer. He said that most of the time, the horses' owners knew most of what was wrong, and his job was to piece the different elements together. This enabled the horses' owners to determine the best things to do to ensure the health and well-being of their charges.

This man came into this field of work by chance. Be began using his pendulum on his household pets. Then friends asked him to work on their pets. Eventually, he found that he had a special affinity with horses and began specializing in that area. He preferred to be with the horse while performing an evaluation, but could also do it from a distance as long as he knew the name of the horse and where it was located.

You may find that you have a natural talent for healing animals with your pendulum. It is a valuable skill, and one that will give you enormous pleasure and satisfaction.

If you would rather not treat your pet yourself, you can use your pendulum to choose the best person to do the job. Write down the names of all the veterinary surgeons in your area and hold your pendulum over each one in turn to determine which one would be best for your pet's needs. Alternatively, you can hold your pendulum and say each name out loud. The pendulum will give a positive indication over the correct name.

You can also use your pendulum to determine the best foods for your pet. At one time we had two cats. When one died, the other almost stopped eating. This was our first experience of this, though our vet told us that it is not uncommon. He prescribed a range of supplements. Unfortunately, Mittens did not like them. I used my pendulum to find similar supplements that our cat would like, and find beneficial.

Obviously, if you are going to use the pendulum for medical purposes you need to know exactly what you are doing. You cannot dabble in this area. Study, observe, and practice. Test everything you do until you are totally proficient. Use your skills as an adjunct to conventional medicine, rather than as an alternative. If you do this, you will be able to help many people with your skills.

chapter six

Into the Psychic

THE PENDULUM IS the perfect instrument to explore the psychic world. It gives us access to both our subconscious and superconscious minds. As such, it is an invaluable tool that can provide added insights to any form of psychic work. For instance, a good friend of mine uses a pendulum whenever he gives a palm reading.

"My client may lie," he says. "But the pendulum always tells the truth."

Just recently, I met an astrologer who uses a pendulum while interpreting horoscope charts.

"I've always used a pendulum to determine people's times of birth," he told me. "I need an accurate time of birth to create the chart in the first place, and the pendulum is wonderful for that. I gradually discovered, and this is not something I'd tell everyone, my pendulum enables me to be more accurate in every way. The chart shows people's potential, for instance, but doesn't tell me how they are using them. Are they capitalizing on their strengths, or simply coasting? The pendulum gives me so much additional information that sometimes I feel I'm a magician, rather than an astrologer."

Psychic Protection with the Pendulum

People have always believed that certain people have the power to harm others using magical or psychic means. If it is possible to heal people from a distance, by sending thoughts of health and well-being, it is certainly possible to send negative energies as well.

Fortunately, most magicians use magic to help others, rather than hurt them. Consequently, the use of supernatural forces to deliberately create a negative outcome is comparatively rare. Although curses are usually topics for fiction writers, they do occur in real life also. Fortunately, you can protect yourself from curses or any other kind of negative force that might be directed toward you.

It is unrealistic to expect everyone to like you. In fact, there are bound to be people who dislike or even hate you. This is a fact of life, and it is best to simply accept it and move on with your own life. One man I know has an interesting slant on this.

"I'd much rather people talked about me behind my back," he says, "Than have them not talk about me at all.

When they talk about me, I matter to them. When I'm ignored, I'm of no account whatsoever."

Talking about you is one thing, attempting to harm you is another matter altogether. Even if you are not aware of anyone wanting to hurt you, you still need to protect yourself, just in case someone attempts to attack you psychically.

A psychic attack might be a deliberate attempt by someone to undermine you. However, it is much more likely to be done subconsciously. There are people known as "psychic vampires" who restore their own energy by draining the energies of other people. I am sure you know people who drain you in this way. After you have spent a short period of time in their company you feel mentally exhausted. These people are psychic vampires. When I made my living as a full-time psychic reader I met more than my share of these unfortunate individuals. I became convinced that some of them were consciously trying to drain my energy, but most do it unknowingly, at least at a conscious level. Get away from these people as quickly as you can. Go out of doors and take several deep breaths of fresh air to restore your body and soul.

As well as this, it is possible that you are being attacked by entities of some sort. Entities are non-physical parasites that attach themselves to humans and create a wide range of physical, mental and emotional problems. They usually attach themselves to people who are in low spirits or ill health, and are least prepared to deal with them.

It is a good idea to ask your pendulum every now and again if you are being attacked psychically. There are a number of occurrences that can give you a clue that you are under attack. You may feel constantly tired and lacking in energy. You may suffer nightmares on a regular basis. Repetitive dreams are another indication. You may suffer from a succession of minor ailments. Your motivation and enthusiasm levels may have decreased.

Whenever anything out of the ordinary occurs you should ask your pendulum to provide the reasons for it. There might be a perfectly logical explanation. For instance, you might become unwell because you have been working too hard and too long without a vacation. In this instance, the remedy is obvious. However, your pendulum might tell you that you have become unwell as a result of a psychic attack.

The Assailant

Your pendulum will be able to tell you where the attack is coming from. It might be from someone who is jealous of your success. It could be someone who resents what you have done. It could even be from a discarnate entity.

Once you have identified the source of the attack, you can ask your pendulum to suggest the best remedies.

A Positive Mental Attitude

The single most important thing you can do to protect yourself from a psychic attack is to maintain a positive attitude towards your life. You can be hurt by a psychic attack only if you allow it to happen. By approaching life in an enthusiastic and positive manner, enjoying the present and working toward specific goals in the future, your mental, physical and emotional selves will be able to withstand any form of psychic attack.

Aura Protection

Your first, and most important, area of defense is your aura. You can strengthen your aura by taking slow deep breaths, inhaling slowly, holding the breath for a few moments, and then exhaling. As you do this, visualize your aura expanding and becoming stronger. You can confirm the size of your aura by asking your pendulum.

Fresh air and sunlight is also extremely beneficial for your aura. You have probably noticed that a brisk walk in the fresh air increases your vitality and energy. It also increases the size of your aura.

Exercise, a massage, and even laughter all increase the size of our auras, and consequently provide psychic protection. Ask your pendulum which activity would be the most beneficial for you while being attacked. Watching comedy shows on television, especially shows that make you laugh out loud, work well for some people, but not for others. These people would benefit more by playing a sport, going to the gym, or enjoying a massage. It is important that the activity is relaxing and enjoyable. I would much rather go for a long walk than work out in the gym. Consequently, the walk is more likely to be beneficial for me in this type of situation than a visit to the gym would be.

It is likely that you will first experience a psychic attack in the bottom four chakras. You should protect these areas whenever you feel negativity coming toward you. You can do this by crossing your arms and legs. If possible, hug a cushion or pillow to provide added protection. Even a book or magazine can be used if you want to protect yourself inconspicuously.

Naturally, when you become aware of this negativity, you should remove yourself from the situation as quickly as you can.

White Light

Protecting your aura is the first, and most vital, area of defense. However, there will be occasions when you desire even more protection. You can increase your level of protection by surrounding yourself with clear white light. Some people picture this as a strong ray of light descending from above and enfolding them in its protection. Other people prefer to visualize it as a circle of light. They can add as many layers of white light as is needed to provide total protection.

White light allows positive energy to get through, but repels all negative energies.

Once you are surrounded by white light, mentally scan your body to see if you are harboring any tension or stress. You can eliminate this by imagining a purple candle in the area of discomfort. The flame of this candle burns up the negative energy, leaving you totally calm, at peace, and in total control.

Like anything else, the more you practice surrounding yourself with white light, the easier it will become. In time, you will be able to surround yourself in white light instantly, simply by saying "white light" to yourself.

It is a good idea to surround yourself in white light whenever you find yourself in a difficult situation. However, it is even better to surround yourself in white light every morning when you wake up. Replenish the white light during the day, if necessary. This means that you will be psychically protected all day long, every single day.

Protecting Your Environment

Frequently, the atmosphere of a house changes when an occupant is the subject of a psychic attack. Fortunately, there are two remedies that can be used.

Ask your pendulum if garlic or salt be used to protect the house. If the pendulum suggests garlic, place a clove of garlic in every room of the house overnight. Gather them all up in the morning and dispose of them. Repeat every night until the attack is over.

If salt is recommended, sprinkle grains of salt in every corner of every room before going to bed. Allow as much fresh air as possible into the house on the following day. Vacuum or sweep up the salt, and replace it before going to bed. Again, repeat this every day until the attack is over.

Magic Circle of Protection

We have already covered everything that is necessary to provide protection from most forms of psychic attack. Occasionally, though, you might need to resort to a more proactive method. A magic circle of protection is ideal for this. You can create a circle anywhere, indoors or out. I know several people who have created circles that included their beds to provide added protection while they were asleep.

You will need a compass to determine east, west, north and south. You may want to draw a circle on the floor, or put down a circular rug to indicate the magic circle. In practice, this is not necessary and I usually imagine the circle to be there.

Stand in the middle of your real or imaginary circle, with your pendulum in your hand. Face the east, with the hand that is holding the pendulum extended. Ask the archangel Raphael for protection.

"Archangel Raphael, I need your help and assistance. Would you please protect me from any harm coming to me from the east."

Wait expectantly, until your pendulum moves to indicate a "yes" response.

Repeat, by turning to the south and asking Michael for protection. Once you have received a positive response, ask the same of Gabriel in the west and Uriel in the north.

After you have received a positive response from all four directions, lower your hand and face the east again. Close your eyes and thank Raphael for coming to your aid. Repeat with the other three archangels.

You should create a circle of protection at least once a day while being attacked. If you make your circle in the same place every time, you will ultimately create a holy place with a peaceful atmosphere that you can sense whenever you venture inside it. Once you reach this state, you need replenish the circle only when you sense that it needs it.

Using Prayer for Protection

Prayers are an extremely effective way of providing psychic protection. Some people feel that if it is to be successful they need to believe in the power of prayer and have a strong faith. However, there are numerous accounts of people throughout history who have cast aside their faith, but prayed for, and received, help and guidance when they needed it.

A prayer does not need to be formal or ritualized. You do not need to kneel, unless you want to. You do not need to go to a church, again unless you want to. A prayer is simply a conversation with God, and you can pray any time you wish.

If you like, you can ask your pendulum if prayer will provide the psychic protection that you require.

Other Types of Protection

Almost anything can be used as a protective talisman to help repel psychic attacks. A cross is a good example. Anything that has been given to you by someone you love will work also. You can also imbue a piece of jewelry or any other object that you regularly carry or wear with you with protective powers. Your pendulum can become a protective talisman in its own right, if you carry it with you all the time.

There is a simple ritual to create protective talismans.

Stand in a place that feels safe and secure. Have the back of your open right hand resting on the palm of your open left hand at about waist height, with the object that is to consecrated resting in your open right palm. (If you are left-handed, rest your left hand on your right palm.)

Close your eyes and surround yourself with white light.

Take several slow deep breaths and allow a feeling of peace and relaxation to flow through your body.

Say to yourself: "I ask the universe to charge this (whatever the object may be) with protective energy to enable me to progress with my life, without fear or worry." If it is possible, say the words out loud and put as much expression into them as possible. By doing this, you will hear the words as you say them. This allows another of your senses to become involved with the ritual.

Within a few seconds you should feel a sensation in the hand that is holding the object. It might be a tingling sensation. The hand may seem warmer, or you may experience a feeling of knowing that the protection has been granted. If you experience nothing at this point, take several deep breaths and go through the ritual again. Sometimes the sensations are extremely subtle, and you need to be acutely aware of them. However, the number of times you go through the ceremony makes no difference, and, in fact, repetition can help.

Once you have noticed the sensation, close your hand over the object and give thanks. "I thank the universe for providing me with the help and protection that I need. Thank you. Thank you. Thank you."

The object is now charged with protective energy and you should wear it or keep it with you at all times. Recharge it whenever you feel it is necessary. You should do it at least once a day when you are experiencing psychic attacks. At other times, recharge it whenever you feel it is time to do so.

The Effect of Belief

Curses and spells depend on the belief of the recipient to work. If you do not believe in the power of a curse, it will not affect you. However, our minds have an immediate and powerful effect on our bodies. Even if you do not believe that a curse or spell will hurt you, you are bound to think about it, and this may have an effect on your body. Consequently, you should take steps to protect yourself, even if you do not believe in the power of the curse or spell.

I know two people who were psychically attacked by a neighbor who objected to the number of pets they had. Justin and Phil are partners in an accountancy practice, and are partners in life also. After a series of confrontations with their neighbor, Justin became ill and became convinced that it was the result of a psychic attack. His pendulum confirmed this to be the case, and also identified the neighbor as the perpetrator. However, Phil did not seem to be affected at all.

During another argument over the fence, the neighbor cursed them both. Justin, who had already been affected by the psychic attack, became depressed and put himself to bed, convinced that he was going to die a slow and painful death. Phil laughed at the curse, but despite his disbelief, began suffering severe headaches. Although he did not believe in the power of the curse, or in the other psychic attacks, his mind kept thinking about it. This ultimately affected his body and created the headaches.

It was as this stage that he decided to take practical steps to protect himself and his partner. Fortunately, it worked. They did not retaliate with curses of their own, but worked at building up a solid wall of psychic protection. When the neighbor learned that his attacks were not working, he gave up and ultimately moved away. Even though he has gone, my acquaintances still regularly protect themselves.

"Whether you believe in it or not," Phil told me, "a psychic attack has the power to hurt you. I didn't believe in it, but the stress I suffered gave me headaches. You have to protect yourself. Why let someone mess up your life, when it's so easy to look after yourself?"

Self-Sabotage

People talk about being attacked psychically by others, but most of us are also guilty of psychically attacking and undermining ourselves. Buried deep inside our subconscious minds are a variety of negative emotions that we have built up over a lifetime, and possibly over many lifetimes.

Your pendulum will tell you what negativity you are holding on to, and will also help you to release it.

Start by asking your pendulum if this negativity is holding you back in any areas of your life. Determine what these areas are by asking your pendulum questions about your work, social life, and family life.

Once you have determined the areas of your life that are involved, discover if you are ready to let go of this negativity by again asking your pendulum. Frequently, people are reluctant to let go of past hurts. Consequently, do not be surprised if you receive a negative answer.

If the pendulum says that you are not ready to let go of the negativity, you need to perform a release ritual.

Hold your pendulum in front of you, and say out loud: "I forgive myself for everything." Repeat these words out loud, over and over again until your pendulum starts moving to indicate your positive response. This may not happen the first few times you do it. Perform this ritual every day until you receive a positive response.

This positive response shows that you can now release the negativity from your subconscious mind.

Go outdoors with your pendulum. Take several deep breaths, holding each breath for a few seconds before exhaling. When you feel ready, say out loud: "I now release all of my negativity. I no longer need it, and I am letting it go. I am letting it go now!"

Repeat these words several times, saying them with as much passion and conviction as you can. You will feel a physical sensation of release as you let the negativity go. One lady I knew who suffered from chronic backache, felt a freeing up sensation in her back, and has had no problems in that area since. Obviously, she was storing her negativity in that part of her body.

After releasing the negativity, pick up your pendulum and ask it if you are still holding on to any negativity. The answer should be "no." If the answer is "yes," repeat the exercise on the following day, and on successive days until your pendulum tells you that all the negativity has gone.

Protection in Daily Life

If you carry your pendulum around with you, you can use it whenever necessary. When you meet someone for the first time, your pendulum will tell you whether or not you can trust him or her. If someone says something to you, your pendulum will be able to tell you if the person is telling the truth.

You can even use the pendulum to determine the character of someone who has sent you a letter. This means that you will know a great deal about this person before even meeting him or her.

Several years ago, a woman consulted me after receiving a series of anonymous letters. She felt she knew who was sending them to her, but the pendulum denied this. She felt that the author of the letters was a woman in her office who was unfriendly and critical. The pendulum told us that the writer of the letters was a man who she had gone out with briefly a couple of years earlier. The pendulum also told us that the woman she suspected was deeply lonely, and her unfriendly manner was a shield she put up around herself to keep people at a distance. Knowing this, my client started talking with this woman and now they are good friends. If the pendulum had not given her this information, she may have wrongly accused her of sending the anonymous letters.

You are not limited to correspondence. A photograph of someone works just as well. You can also hold your pendulum over any object belonging to someone else, and ask it questions about the owner of the item.

By doing this, you will be able to protect yourself from people who are dishonest or mean harm.

Telepathy with the Pendulum

Telepathy is the ability of two people to be able to communicate without using the normal five senses. The ability of a mother to know when something is wrong with one of her children, no matter where in the world he or she may be, is an example of this. Telepathy can be planned or spontaneous. There are many recorded examples of someone who has just died contacting a friend or relative at the moment of death to say goodbye. There are also many documented instances of people sitting down in different rooms with the intention of communicating with each other using their sixth sense.

Let us assume that you need to contact someone urgently. You have no idea where he or she is, so you cannot use the phone or e-mail. However, you can use your pendulum.

Sit down somewhere with your pendulum and focus on the person you wish to contact. Look at a photograph of the person while doing this, if you have one. A photograph is not essential, but it makes it easier to tune in on the person you are seeking. You might want to write the person's name down on a piece of paper, but again, this is not essential.

Concentrate on the person you are trying to contact. Ask him or her to contact you immediately. Focus on the person until your pendulum starts giving strong positive movements. This is a sign that contact has been made. Again, ask the person to contact you right away, and then relax. If you have been successful, the person you are trying to find will contact you.

Repeat this process as many times as you wish until contact has been made. Realize that the person may have received your message, but be unable to contact you. Be patient, and remain confident that he or she will do so as soon as it is possible.

Divination with the Pendulum

People have always been fascinated with the future. This is why fortunetellers are usually busy people. I frequently use my pendulum in conjunction with other forms of divination. One of my favorite methods involves dominoes.

Dominoes originated in China and were used for divination purposes as well as a parlor game. They were introduced into Europe in the early eighteenth century and quickly became popular for gaming purposes. The name domino probably derives from a black cloak called a domino, as early sets were made of ebony with ivory faces.[1]

The dominoes are placed face downward on a table and thoroughly mixed. Some people feel that the domino furthest away from you should be chosen, but others say that you should let your psychic hand guide you to a particular domino. (Your psychic hand is your left hand if you are right-handed, and the right if you are left-handed.) I prefer to let my pendulum choose a domino for me.

To do this, slowly pass your pendulum over each of the dominoes until you receive a positive reaction. It might be a pulling sensation, or your pendulum may start giving a positive indication. That is the domino to choose.

Usually, one domino is enough to answer a question. However, in domino lore it is permitted to select up to three dominoes at a session. One domino is chosen and interpreted and then replaced with the others. The dominoes are then thoroughly mixed before a second domino is chosen. The same procedure applies for the third domino, if it is needed. Consequently, it is possible, though most unlikely, to pick the same domino three times. It is considered extremely auspicious if the same domino is chosen twice. If this occurs, the pendulum can select a fourth domino.

Tradition says you should not consult the dominoes more than once a month, and should not consult them on a Monday or Friday. The lady who taught me domino readings thought that they should not be read more than once a week, and did not care which day of the week it was. She felt that they should be used whenever necessary, because problems can arise on any day of the week.

Although I am listing the meanings for each domino here, allow your intuition to be your guide. By doing this, you will gradually create your own interpretations, and these will usually be more accurate for you and the people around you. Ask your pendulum to confirm your findings. You will also find that when you read the standard interpretations of the dominoes you will often create psychic impressions in your mind. These feelings and impressions will always be correct.

The hardest part when you are first starting is to trust your first impressions. This is something that comes with practice. One technique that many people find helpful is to relax or meditate for a short while before starting the divination. This allows you to slow down all the myriad thoughts that constantly crowd everyone's minds, and make true intuitive flashes hard to recognize.

The meanings for each domino are:

Double blank. This is the least auspicious domino. It means that you should take care of your money and possessions. Beware of theft and loss.

One blank. A stranger could provide help or information. You will be happy with the news. Be prepared to move forward. Do not hold back unnecessarily.

One-one. This indicates happiness in love and marriage. It promises harmony and peace of mind. It also relates to financial security.

Two-blank. This domino relates to misfortune and bad luck. If a woman chooses this domino, the misfortune relates to a male in her life. Oddly enough, this is a highly auspicious domino if you are planning to travel.

Two-one. This is a fortunate domino. It indicates love and marriage for single women, and a fun-filled time for single men. It suggests caution in business.

Two-two. This is an excellent domino that indicates happiness, harmony, and success at home and in business. Some unexpected news will bring great joy.

Three-blank. This domino indicates disagreements. Stand up for yourself, but avoid antagonizing others. Be sure of your facts before opening your mouth.

Three-one. This domino is an indication to avoid gossip, and the company of people who constantly put others down. Make friends with positive-minded people, and avoid flatterers.

Three-two. This domino indicates good fortune in love, family life, and career. It is a good time to travel.

Three-three. This domino is an indication of money coming your way. You are likely to receive recognition for what you have done.

Four-blank. This domino indicates a disappointment. Do not reveal too much to others. Think carefully before moving ahead.

Four-one. This is an indication of future prosperity and immediate happiness. You can make new friends now, as long as you are prepared to make the first move.

Four-two. This domino indicates a change is in store. Be particularly careful with money matters, and avoid any extravagances. Avoid people you do not trust.

Four-three. This domino promises a happy life. Share your thoughts and feelings with others. Respect other people's confidences.

Four-four. This domino indicates a time for happiness and laughter. It is good for social activities, making new friends, and spending time with loved ones. It indicates a slow period as far as work and career are concerned.

Five-blank. This domino is an indication to seek advice from someone who may be able to resolve a problem, or answer a specific question. Think first. Do not take any unnecessary risks.

Five-one. This domino indicates a busy and happy social life. You have the potential to progress in your career as long as you pay attention to all the details.

Five-two. This domino counsels caution. Do not rush into anything, as you might make a decision you later regret. Think carefully before acting.

Five-three. This domino indicates a slow, but steady, improvement financially. It marks a busy time at work. Take time off when possible to relax and unwind.

Five-four. This domino indicates caution in investments. Take professional advice when necessary, and do not allow yourself to become overextended.

Five-five. This domino is a sign of success in all things. You are likely to make the right decisions, and be appreciated by others.

Six-blank. This domino is usually considered an unhappy one. It can portend a death, but usually it is a sign that something is ending to make way for the new. You may find yourself the subject of malicious gossip.

Six-one. This is a sign of success in relationships. Be attentive to the needs of younger family members, and be prepared to listen. Give advice only if it is asked for. This domino can be an indicator of a second marriage.

Six-two. This domino is excellent for people who are honest. It is a sign that their fortunes will improve. It indicates that dishonest people will get caught out.

Six-three. This is a very auspicious domino for love and for money. It indicates a time to ask for what you want.

Six-four. This domino indicates a happy and contented home and family life. A younger family member might seek advice.

Six-five. This domino indicates that hard work, determination and persistence will pay off. Do not give up.

Six-six. This domino relates to speculation, and indicates that you can take a chance with a strong likelihood of success. Trust your feelings.

Telephone Readings

A friend of mine in Los Angeles worked for one of the 1-900 psychic phone lines for a couple of years. She always used her pendulum. It allowed her to tune in to the callers and resolve their problems more efficiently and accurately than she could when she used clairvoyance alone.

You can do the same. If a friend calls you with a problem, you can ask your pendulum for the answers. It works just as well over the phone as it does when your friend is sitting beside you.

You must be sympathetic, understanding, and gentle when you are dealing with people over the phone. However, do not let people call you every time they have a slight problem. Let them work these out for themselves. Save your pendulum for the occasions when you feel it would be most beneficial and useful.

Pendulum Numerology

Numerology is one of the oldest of the divinatory arts. It began in China many thousands of years ago, and reached Europe at least three thousand years ago. Pythagoras "modernized" the art some twenty-six-hundred years ago.

This is an effective way of predicting the outcome of a future event. You will need nine cards and nine opaque envelopes to put them in. Write the number "one" on the first card and place it into an envelope. Continue in the same way with the numbers up to nine.

Think of the question you wish to ask. You can ask any sort of question. It does not have to have worldwide implications. You can ask a question about world peace, if you want, but you can also ask questions about the chances of rain tomorrow. While thinking of your question, mix the envelopes thoroughly until you have no idea which number is in any of them.

Deal the nine envelopes in a row in front of you. Think about your question, and desire for an answer, while you suspend your pendulum over each of the envelopes in turn. It will react in a different manner over one of the envelopes. Usually, this will be your positive response. The pendulum will give little or no reaction over the other envelopes.

Open up the envelope. The number inside will be the answer to your question.

Here are the interpretations for each number:

One This a time for new starts. Everything is going your way at present. Aim high and set big, worthwhile goals.

Two Patience will be rewarded. This is not a time to push or to force your will on others. Think, prepare, socialize, and wait for indications to move ahead.

Three This is a good time for social activities, hobbies, and less-serious pursuits. Do the work that is required, but allow time for relaxation also.

Four This is a sign of slow, steady progress. You may feel hemmed in and limited, but the hard work you do now pays off.

Five This is the perfect time to change anything. The only constant in life is change. Resolve to make these changes the ones that you want.

Six Home and family responsibilities are emphasized. You may find yourself doing things for others, rather than for yourself. Enjoy the pleasures of giving.

Seven This is a time to think, to meditate, and to learn. It is not a time for material progress. Make plans, and wait until you receive a sign to put them into action.

Eight This is a time of hard work, but it will pay off. Money matters will go your way, also. Make sure to allow some time for relaxation.

Nine This is a time to replace anything that has outworn its use. You are likely to find it hard to let go, but it is essential. You will also be making plans for the future.

Sometimes the answers are obvious, but at other times you will have to think about them. Let us assume that you asked if you were going to get a pay increase at work. If the pendulum indicated numbers one and eight, you would be practically guaranteed a pay increase. However, it is doubtful that you would receive it in the near future if the pendulum indicated numbers two or seven. Number three would tend to indicate that you were coming into a fun time, but that a pay increase was not part of it. Four definitely indicates a pay increase, but that you would be faced with more hard work or increased responsibilities. A five would indicate a change in the nature of your work. This might be connected with the work you are currently doing, or may be a complete change of occupation. A six would indicate that something at home is currently more important that a pay increase, and that this should be attended to first. Finally, a nine indicates that you have to let go of something before starting anything new. Whatever this is needs to be attended to first, before asking for a raise in pay.

Exploring Your Past Lives

The pendulum is a useful tool in exploring your previous incarnations. There are many ways of discovering and examining your past lives.[2] The pendulum is slow and laborious compared to some of the other methods, but it has the advantage of being highly specific. In many hypnotic past-life regressions, for instance, people do not know their dates of birth and death, and frequently do not know the name of the country they were living in. It is a simple matter for the pendulum to provide this sort of information.

Step 1: When Were You Last Here?

Hold your pendulum and ask it if you were born in the twentieth century in your most recent past life. Keep going back, century by century, until you receive a positive response.

Ask your pendulum if you were born in the first half of that century. If the answer is negative, it obviously means that you were born in the second half of the century. Ask your pendulum if this is the case. This confirms that you are doing everything correctly.

Next, ask about specific decades, and then start on individual years, until you determine your year of birth.

Naturally, you can continue to find out your month and day of birth as well. Most of the time, I do not bother with this, and come back to find it only if I need it later on.

Step 2: Where Did You Live?

If you have a feeling that you were born in a certain place, start by asking your pendulum if that was the case. Otherwise, you need to go through the alphabet, asking if the country you were born in began with an "A," a "B," and so on.

Once you find the first letter, you need to repeat the process with as many other letters as are necessary to determine the name of the country.

Occasionally, the name of a town or region will come up when doing this exercise. If you were born in the Algarve region of France in your past life, you might think you were born in Algeria after working out the first few letters.

Step 3: Were You Male or Female?

This step is an easy one to do. All the same ask the pendulum about both male and female, as this helps to check your progress.

Step 4: What Was Your Name?

Again you need to go through the alphabet to determine your name, one letter at a time. Sometimes you can speed this process up. If your pendulum spells out J-O-N, you should ask it if your name was Jonathan. This can save quite a bit of time if you are correct.

Step 5: How Did You Spend Your Time?

You can go through the alphabet to determine your occupation. I prefer to start by asking about occupations that were likely to be popular in the time and place that I am examining. You could ask if you were involved in agriculture, fishing, healing, teaching and so on. Again, this saves time if you are correct. If I am unsuccessful after several guesses, I will work my way through the alphabet.

Step 6: Who From This Life Was With You in the Previous Life?

It is common for groups of people to be reincarnated together. This is especially the case with close relatives and friends. The relationships and sexes change, but the souls of special people in this lifetime are likely to have been with you in a number of previous incarnations. Your sister in this lifetime might have been your son or mother last time. Changes of sex are common and are designed to allow us to experience every aspect of life.

I always ask about my parents, wife, and children. Sometimes I extend that to other close relatives and a few friends.

Step 7: Did You Have a Family?

At this stage, I ask if I was married. I also find out how many children I had. I ask questions about their sexes, health, and well-being.

Step 8: What Were You Like?

Now you can start asking questions about yourself. Were you rich? Famous? Popular? Successful? Loved by others? Healthy? What did you enjoy doing in your leisure time? Were you lonely in your old age?

Step 9: When Did You Die?

I used to ask my pendulum if I was old when I died, thinking that this might save time. However, the pendulum sometimes gave strange answers. The pendulum might say that I was old when I actually died at the age of forty-four. However, in terms of the life I was exploring, that was old.

Now I start by asking if I was over fifty when I died. If the answer was "yes," I ask if I was over sixty, and move ahead a decade at a time until I receive a negative response. I then move ahead one year at a time from the age given in the last positive response to determine the exact age.

Naturally, if the pendulum said I was not over fifty, I do the same process in reverse, going back a decade at a time.

Step 10: What Karma Affects You This Lifetime?

Before leaving this past life you can find out what karma you built up in that lifetime that is affecting you in your current life.

Start by asking if there are karmic debts relating to this previous life. Find out what area of your life they are in, by asking if they relate to work, relationships, lust, greed, avarice, and so on.

Ask the pendulum if it is possible to repay this debt in your current life. Keep on asking questions until you determine what you can do. Finally, work on them until they are repaid. You can check with your pendulum every now and again to find out how you are progressing.

As you can see, this is a lengthy process. In fact, when I do this, it usually takes even longer than what I have described here. That is because I ask all sorts of questions along the way to clarify and amplify the lifetime as much as possible. I might want the exact dates of birth and death. I might want to know details about my parents, brothers and sisters, children and friends. I might want to learn about my education. There is no limit to the number of questions that can be asked.

Once you have learned as much as you want to know about this past life, you might want to go back further and explore another one. I know from experience that experiments like this can become extremely addictive.

Communicating with Ghosts

A member of a club I belong to moved into a new house. Gerald and his wife, Natalie, were excited about it, as they were moving from a modest home to a large, expensive home overlooking the city. A few weeks after they moved in, I asked him how they were enjoying their new home.

"It's hard to say," he replied. "We love the house, and everything about it. Well, except for just one thing. The dining room feels cold and unpleasant all the time." He laughed nervously. "Natalie thinks it might be haunted."

This caught my attention. "Could I come and see it?" I asked. "If it's haunted, I might be able to help."

He grabbed my arm. "Would you, please?"

I called on them the following evening. Gerald and Natalie took me on a tour of the house, leaving the dining room until last. It had been a hot, sunny summer's day, and the entire house was warm, except for the dining room. The energies of this room were totally different.

I took my pendulum out and held it in front of me.

"Is there anyone there?" I asked.

The pendulum remained motionless for perhaps thirty seconds, and then gave a positive response.

"Can I help you?" I asked. Again, the pendulum gave a positive response.

"Is this your home?" My pendulum told me: Yes.

It took about half an hour to figure out that the spirit was that of a young man. He had been killed in a horseriding accident, just three weeks before his wedding day. All of this had happened sixty years ago. The young man meant no harm.

"Are you unable to move on?" I asked.

The young man replied that he was able to move on, but did not want to. He was twenty-one at the time of his death and felt that he had missed out on all that life had to offer.

"You are missing out now," I told him. "You should be progressing and moving forward. You are not fulfilling your soul's purpose by remaining here. Do you understand that?"

My pendulum told me that he understood.

"Are you ready to let go now?"

There was a long pause before my pendulum gave the "I do not want to answer" response.

I told him about the new couple who had moved into the house, and how happy they were. They would look after the house well. Wasn't it time for him to let go, and let the new people take over? My pendulum gave an extremely faint "yes." (This means that the positive response from my pendulum was a weak, rather than a strong movement.)

I introduced him to Gerald and Natalie. They had been standing in the doorway, with their arms around each other's waists the whole time I had been communicating with the spirit. Now they came into the room and stood beside me.

"Hello," Gerald said.

"Tell him what you are planning to do with the house," I suggested.

Gerald looked embarrassed at the thought of talking to a ghost.

"I'll tell him," Natalie said. She cleared her throat. "We love this house," she said. "When I was a young girl, I used to look up at this house and tell myself that I'd live in it one day. It was a dream. I never thought it would happen. Gerry and I have worked really hard for years to get here. The house needs a bit of work. We are going to do that. It will be a labor of love for us. We plan to stay here for many, many years. This house is going to be full of love and happiness. In a few weeks two of our grandchildren are coming to stay. I know they'll love this house just as much as Gerry and me. It's our home."

When she stopped talking, Gerald began. "Developers wanted this piece of land," he said. "They were going to tear this house down and build a whole lot of apartments. We would never do that. We love everything about this place."

"Can you let go?" I asked. This time the positive response was much stronger.

"Thank you," I said.

The following evening I returned to the house. There was no noticeable difference between the energies of the dining room and that of any of the other rooms. Natalie was a little concerned that we had cast a ghost out of his home, but brightened when I told her that he was now free to move forward to the next stage of his development.

Many people use the pendulum to communicate with ghosts. What we call ghosts or spirits are not the unpleasant, malevolent entities that movies sometimes depict. There is no need to be afraid of them. In my experience, they enjoy conversing with others. The pendulum is an effective way of communicating with them. I also know people who use pendulums to track down ghosts, but have not done this myself.

Dream Recall

Dreams can be incredibly frustrating. It is annoying to wake up after a dream and have it fade from your memory before you have had a chance to think about it. People who cannot remember their dreams sometimes feel that they do not dream at all. This is not the case. We all have four to five periods of dreaming every time we have a good night's sleep.

In our sleep we drift through different stages of consciousness. About ninety minutes after falling asleep we enter the first dream stage. Scientists have observed that this stage is characterized by rapid eye movements, a partial paralysis of the muscles, and the stimulation of erectile tissue in both men and women.

This first dream stage lasts between ten and twenty minutes, and then a deeper stage of sleep begins. This lasts about ninety minutes, and then the dream stage starts again. Consequently, in the course of six hours sleep we would experience four dream stages.

If you happen to wake up normally, it will be directly after one of these dream stages. This may not be the case, of course, if an alarm clock, a noise, or someone else wakes you.

Consequently, you are most likely to remember your dreams on those occasions when you wake up naturally, and are able to lie in bed for a while before getting up. Even on those occasions, though, there will be times when you cannot recall anything of the dream you have just had.

Fortunately, your pendulum can help. Hold your pendulum and say to it: "I know I dreamt last night, but I can remember nothing about it. Will you help me?"

Wait for a positive response, and then ask it the following questions:

"Did my dream include my wife/husband/significant other?"

"Did my dream involve my working life?"

"Did my dream involve my hobby of (whatever it may be)?"

"Did my dream involve (sport, hobby, or any other important interest)?"

Frequently, the answer to one of these questions will trigger a partial memory. This might be all you need to recall the dream.

If you do not receive enough information from these questions, say the following emotional words and see how your pendulum reacts:

> Cat, dog, house, car, lover, wife, husband, child, career, money, sex, travel, fear, success, sport, action, adventure, flying, health, accident.

If you can remember some of your previous dreams, add keywords from them to the list and see what reaction they receive from your pendulum. Gradually, your dream will take shape and the forgotten memories will return.

It is a good idea to keep a dream diary by your bed. Write down your memories of your dreams as soon as possible after you wake up. I find that memories often return if I tell someone about the dream. Naturally, I write down in my dream diary anything that comes back.

The dream diary is also useful as a source of emotional words that can be used with the pendulum. Also, if all else fails, you can suspend your pendulum over the accounts of previous dreams and ask if the dream you are trying to remember was similar in nature.

chapter seven

Color and the Pendulum

People have been experimenting with color and the pendulum for at least one hundred years. In the early part of the twentieth century, a French professor called Henri Mager devised a color wheel known as Mager's Rosette.[1] This was a circle divided into eight equal segments, each painted a different color. The colors he used were: violet, blue, green, yellow, red, gray, black, and white. The violet segment was placed at the top, and the other colors followed in a clockwise direction. To use the Mager's Rosette, the violet segment has to face north. This placed green in the east, red in the south and black in the west. If you suspend your pendulum over each color in turn, you will receive a positive response on violet, green, red and black segments, but no response on the others. (Professor Mager used large rosettes, two or three feet in diameter, and usually used a dowsing rod instead of a pendulum. Naturally, much smaller rosettes can be used with a pendulum.)

Henri Mager believed that there were strong bonds between certain colors and substances. If he wanted to find out which color had an affinity with silver, for instance, he would place it on each segment of his rosette in turn, and then test to see if he received a positive response from the four directions. Let us assume that the piece of silver is placed in the grey segment. Professor Mager would hold his pendulum over each segment in turn, and discover no reaction from the colors marking north, south, east, and west. However, when he placed the piece of silver in the black segment, he would receive a positive response from these segments, telling him that there is a strong affinity between silver and the color black.

This is an interesting experiment, but one that you would think had little practical use. However, it means that if you are using your pendulum to find silver, and want a small sample of it to help the process, you could use anything that is black in color instead. Some dowsers have even gone to the trouble of painting their pendulums the correct color for the object they are dowsing for. Consequently, if you were searching for copper, you could paint your pendulum dark violet, as that is the color that has an affinity with copper. Likewise, red is the color to use when searching for iron.

I have not found the need to do this myself, as I focus on whatever it is I am dowsing for, and let the pendulum locate it for me. However, you might like to experiment with it, and see how well it works for you.

Probably the most magical form of color is the rainbow. I know that rainbows are formed by light playing on raindrops, and are a purely natural phenomenon, but just like William Wordsworth, "My heart leaps up when I behold,/ A rainbow in the sky." Isn't there something magical in the fact that you can never reach a rainbow? If you try to catch a rainbow, it continues to move away.

In Chapter Five we discussed the chakras and the colors related to each one. All of us are living rainbows, as we are each expressing all seven colors through our chakras.

However, it is rare for anyone to express him or herself equally through all seven colors. In most people one or two of the colors predominate at the expense of the others. This is not necessarily a bad thing as the strongest colors give clues about the person's approach to life and the type of career he or she would be best suited for.

All the same, the ultimate goal is to achieve a balance, in which all the colors are used. People like this are said to be well-balanced or "centered."

You may instinctively know what colors are strongest in your makeup. If you love playing sports and enjoy all physical activities you are bound to be strong in red energy. If you enjoy mentally stimulating activities, there will be a strong blue element in your makeup.

There are a variety of ways of determining your strongest colors. You may be able to work out which colors relate best to you from the following descriptions of each color.

Red

People with a strong red component enjoy physical activities. They are motivated, enthusiastic people who have a great deal of inner strength and leadership potential. They are also emotional and passionate. These people have strong personal needs and will do whatever is necessary to achieve them. They prefer to go their own way and work best in situations where they are left to get on with the task, with no one telling them what to do.

Red is exciting, stimulating and energizing. Focussing on anything red, or even thinking about the color, can give you energy when you are feeling tired.

Orange

People with a strong orange component are sensitive to the feelings and needs of others. They are cooperative, considerate, and friendly. They are naturally good at making people feel welcome. They are born diplomats and peacemakers. They can be extremely persuasive, and use tact and charm to achieve their aims. They are cheerful, warm and tolerant. However, they are also sensitive and can be easily hurt as a result.

Orange provides peace.

Yellow

People with a strong yellow component are sociable, creative, and outgoing. They have an empathy with words and enjoy expressing themselves verbally. They have good minds and love new ideas and concepts. They are imaginative and creative, but sometimes lack motivation. They are positive and bounce back quickly after any setbacks. They love mixing with others and usually enjoy themselves everywhere they go.

Yellow stimulates the mental faculties.

Green

People with a strong green component are hard-working, practical, down-to-earth, determined and conscientious. They are prepared to work hard to achieve their goals. They are patient and good with the details. They enjoy system, order, and routine. They can be stubborn, rigid, and fixed in their approach to life.

Green is soothing and healing.

Blue

People with a strong blue component are versatile, enthusiastic and mentally alert. They see opportunities everywhere. They enjoy freedom, change and variety, and hate feeling restricted or hemmed in. They have a need to learn, to know, and to understand. They have the potential to motivate and inspire others.

Blue is the perfect antidote to mental strain.

Indigo

People with a strong indigo component are loving, sympathetic, generous and kind. They enjoy responsibility and experience great pleasure in helping and serving others. If they say they will do something, they will do it. They are idealistic, tolerant, and understanding. They are happiest when in love, and when surrounded by loved ones. Home and family are the prime focus of their lives. They are intuitive, spiritual, and have a strong awareness that we are both spiritual and physical beings.

Violet

People with a strong violet component are intuitive, aware, and spiritual. They search for hidden truths and want to know and understand everything. They want a perfect world, and consequently are frequently disappointed. They are refined, sensitive, understanding, and wise. They are reserved and discriminating. They need a great deal of time on their own to meditate, and grow in knowledge and wisdom.

Violet soothes and calms the nerves, and aids spiritual development.

Which Are Your Colors?

You may have recognized yourself in the descriptions of each color. This will be the case if you are living most of the time in the realms of one or two of the colors. If you are engaged in physical activities most of the time, you will have a strong red component in your makeup. If you are engaged in research, you are more likely to be expressing blue. Of course, we are all mixtures of every color, and your pendulum will be able to tell you which are your strongest colors.

To do this, go through the colors one by one, asking if each one is your strongest color. Your pendulum will tell you which one you are expressing most strongly.

You can then repeat this by asking for your second strongest color. If you want, you can determine the strength of each color in the same way.

How Good a Rainbow Are You?

It is a good idea to regularly ask your pendulum about all the colors in your makeup. By doing this, you can restore the colors that you are deficient in. Sometimes you will be aware of a deficiency. If you have been overexerting yourself, for instance, you will probably be low on red. However, there are also times when you feel that you are not one hundred percent, but have no idea what is wrong.

The easiest way to find out is to ask your pendulum about each color. "Do I have sufficient quantities of red in my makeup?" and so on.

I prefer to do this by asking these questions while suspending my pendulum over pieces of cardboard that depict the seven colors of the rainbow. Then, if my pendulum indicates that any color is low or depleted, I can focus on the color immediately.

Hold your pendulum over the color and say out loud: "I am restoring my levels of (whatever color is required)." Your pendulum will start to move in your positive direction for thirty to sixty seconds and then stop. This is an indication that your levels are back to normal. If you want, you can check this by going through the colors again, asking if you have sufficient quantities of each.

An alternative method of restoring your levels of any color are to stare at the color for a few minutes, while taking slow deep breaths. Each time you inhale, imagine that you are bringing in quantities of the color.

Another method is to close your eyes and imagine that you are being bathed in a bath of the color that you are deficient in.

You can also drink the color that you need. Again, there are a number of ways of doing this.

The first is to place a glass of water on a table. Place the palm of your right hand (left if you are left-handed) a couple of inches above the glass. Imagine your body full to overflowing with the color that you need. Visualize it coming down your arm and through the palm of your hand into the glass of water. Picture this for as long as you can, and then drink the water.

Another method uses a glass that is the same color as the one you need. Alternatively, you can wrap a clear glass in cellophane of the right color. Place this in the sunlight for several minutes, and then drink it. If you do not have any cellophane, wrap the glass in material of the correct color. Place it outside when the sun first gets up, and leave it there for a few hours. You can prepare several jugs of water at the same time, if you wish. Store them in the refrigerator until you are ready to drink them.

If you experiment with this, you will discover that each color has a different taste.

We experimented with this in my psychic development classes. Most of the students enjoyed the taste of blue, although a few found it metallic. Most found red, orange, and yellow to have an "earthy" taste. Some liked it, all the same. Green seemed to be neutral, while indigo and violet seemed pure and fresh.

Rainbow Meditation

It is always beneficial to see a rainbow, as we are instantly presented with all seven colors. Usually, a rainbow makes us pause briefly in our daily routine, and that is good for us, also. However, we do not need to actually see a rainbow to experience these benefits. It is possible to walk through a rainbow anytime you wish, simply by closing your eyes and taking yourself through a rainbow meditation.

Sit down comfortably, close your eyes, and take several deep breaths. Allow your body to relax.

When you feel ready, visualize a rainbow in your mind. It makes no difference if you can see the rainbow, sense it, feel it, or simply know that it is there.

Imagine yourself walking up to the rainbow. Feel the sense of anticipation you experience when you realize that you are about to walk inside this gorgeous, multicolored rainbow.

Pause for a moment, and then walk into the red band of the rainbow. Feel it, sense it, experience it. See the misty red light that completely surrounds and enfolds you. Feel the stimulating, energizing effects of the red as it reaches into every fiber of your being.

Stand in the red band for as long as you wish, and then move on to the orange. You may experience a tingling sensation as you move further into the orange ray. Pause once you are completely surrounded by this orange mist. Enjoy the restorative effects of this pure orange. Allow it to reach into every part of your body.

When you feel ready, move on to the yellow band. Notice how the misty hues become finer and finer the further you walk into this magnificent rainbow. Feel the purity of the yellow as it surrounds you and penetrates into every particle of your being.

Stay in the yellow ray for as long as you wish, and then move into the green band. Feel yourself being totally bathed and revitalized by the wonderful healing qualities of the green. Allow any stress or strain to wash away as you pause and enjoy the gentle, restorative qualities of this pure green.

As you walk from the green into the blue, you might notice a trace of pure turquoise. And now you are surrounded by blue energy. Feel the insight and clarity of mind that you experience as you stand in the center of the blue ray. Enjoy the mental stimulation and the sense of calmness and confidence that tells you that you can accomplish anything you set your mind upon.

Make the most of this pure blue before stepping into the indigo band. The division between the two is extremely subtle, but you are aware of the changes in your mind and body as you pause in the center of the indigo ray.

Spend time enjoying the special qualities of indigo before moving into the final ray, violet. Experience your heightened intuitions. Feel the limitless of your healing potential. Open your mind to inspiration. Enjoy the peace and tranquillity that comes from immersing yourself in the purity of the violet ray.

When you feel ready, walk out of the rainbow, but keep your eyes closed for a minute or two. Reflect on what you experienced. Mentally scan your body to see what physical changes have occurred. Silently give thanks, before opening your eyes, and carrying on with your day.

It is not necessary to do the entire meditation. If your pendulum tells you that you are deficient in, say, yellow, you can visualize yourself walking into the yellow ray and experiencing all of the benefits that come from immersing yourself in yellow.

You may find that you can visualize the rainbow and enter into it anywhere. Your body will tell you which colors you need any time you do this. You might be surprised to find that the colors you need vary from day to day.

Dowsing the Aura

The chakras embody all the colors of the rainbow, and make up an important part of the aura. The aura is an energy field that surrounds all living things. People tend to think that it surrounds the body, but it should be considered as an extension of the body. The aura is alive with color, but most people do not see it. However, with practice, anyone can learn how to see the colors in the aura.[2]

You can use your pendulum to determine the size of the energy fields surrounding anyone.

Ask a friend to stand with his or her arms and legs slightly apart. Move thirty feet away. Slowly walk toward your friend, with your pendulum in your hand. At some stage, the pendulum will start to react. Usually, it will start to gyrate, but it can give other reactions. This is an indication that you have reached the outer edge of your friend's aura.

If you keep on moving forward, you will find that the pendulum experiences a slight resistance before entering the aura. The aura is made up of a number of layers, and your pendulum will indicate each time you reach one of these.

This is an interesting test, and you will probably be surprised at how large your friend's aura is. Experiment at different times of day, and also when your friend is both fresh and tired. You will find that the aura expands and contracts according to the physical and emotional states of the person.

How to Determine the Colors of the Aura

When people start seeing auras, they usually see them as slightly grayish clouds of energy. Gradually, the colors become visible, and eventually they glow with life and energy. When this stage is reached, you will wonder how you never saw them before.

There are many colors in the aura. The most important of these is the ground color, which reveals what the person should be doing with his or her life. Your pendulum will be able to tell you what color your ground color is. Start by asking the pendulum about each color in the rainbow. If it gives a negative reaction to each of these, ask if your ground color is silver, gold, pink, bronze, or white.

If your ground color is red, you should be learning to stand on your own two feet and achieve independence.

If your ground color is orange, you should be tactful, intuitive, and have a gift for making other people feel at ease.

If your ground color is yellow, you should be expressing yourself in some way, ideally in a creative way.

If your ground color is green, you should be peace-loving, generous, hard-working, and a natural healer. You are also likely to be stubborn.

If your ground color is blue, you should be positive, enthusiastic, adventurous, and enjoy change and variety in your life.

If your ground color is indigo, you should be friendly, loving, responsible, and caring.

If your ground color is violet, you should enjoy learning hidden truths. You should be developing inwardly, and growing in knowledge and wisdom.

If your ground color is silver, you should have access to great ideas, and have the potential to achieve them. This ground color is rare.

If your ground color is gold, you have the potential to achieve anything. You should aim high, plan carefully, and then move forward and make a difference in the world.

If your ground color is pink, you should be making material progress in this incarnation. You are likely to be rigid in outlook, and this can hold you back.

If your ground color is bronze, you should be caring, philanthropic, and a natural humanitarian.

If your ground color is white, you should be pure, modest, and have the potential to help and inspire others. Like silver, this ground color is rare.[3]

Radiating Colors

The meanings of the ground colors are modified by colors that radiate outward through the aura. Not surprisingly, these colors are known as radiating colors. Most people have one or two pronounced radiating colors, though it is possible to have a complete rainbow of radiating colors. Again, your pendulum will be able to tell you what your radiating colors are.

Polarity

While you are measuring your friend's aura, you can also check his or her polarity. If you hold your pendulum close to your friend's right side, you will find that your pendulum gyrates in a clockwise manner. This indicates a positive polarity. However, when you hold it next to his or her left side, you will find that it gyrates in a counterclockwise manner, revealing negative polarity.

After working with colors for a short while, you will understand why colors are used so often in everyday speech. People really do become red with rage, green with envy, and feel the blues. I've been accused of seeing the world through rose-colored glasses. Color and the pendulum make a powerful combination.

chapter eight

Pendulum Magic Divination Ritual

THE PENDULUM IS a magical tool that can be used anywhere, at any time. Because it is such a powerful magic tool, many people like to use it as part of a ritual, especially when they are undertaking white magic. White magic seeks its goals through worship and offerings to whichever god is being invoked. This form of ritual releases powerful cosmic forces that fill the magician with energy and power. This enables him or her to manifest whatever is being requested.

A rite is a formal practice. A ritual is a series of actions, or rites, performed in a prescribed manner. It could be as simple as saying a magic word, or it might be a lengthy, formalized process that takes an hour or more. When a ritual is performed properly, magic will happen. This is why you need to be properly prepared and focussed whenever performing a ritual of any sort.

Throughout history, people in every part of the world have performed rituals to achieve their goals. Fertility rites and rituals to make rain are common examples. Ceremonial magic is full of powerful rituals.

Divination is a form of magic that allows us to part the veil into the future and glimpse within. With practice, anyone can do it. Each time you practice, you develop your skills of intuition. Learning to trust your first impressions is an important part of the process.

This is a simple ritual that anyone can do. I know many people who have experienced great success with it. If you are experienced in ritual magic you can add to it, perhaps by including opening and closing ceremonies, involving the invoking and banishing rituals of the pentagram. Alternatively, you might wish to use this as part of a larger ritual.

No matter what you do, keep the ritual as simple and uncomplicated as possible. Many magicians feel that real magic is hard to do, and that traditional, involved rituals are the only way to effect change. This is not necessarily true. If you perform your rituals with the right aims in mind, you can achieve your goals simply, easily and without great effort.

Ritual Requirements

You will need somewhere private to hold the ritual. A room in your home is fine, but make sure that you will not be interrupted until the ritual is complete. The room should be as clean as possible. At the very least, sweep or vacuum the room before starting. It is a good idea to remove any clutter in the room.

The first thing you will need is a magic altar. Almost anything can be used for this. A small table or anything with a solid, flat surface will do. Place the altar so that you will be facing east when working on it. The sun rises in the east, making this a positive direction to face when performing white magic. You should cover the altar with a white cloth. This cloth should be purchased specifically for this purpose and used only as an altar cloth. Pure silk is considered the best material for this, but any white cloth will do. You can embroider or decorate the cloth in other ways, if you wish.

You will need a magic circle to work in. Your altar should fit inside this circle. The ideal size for a magic circle is about six or seven feet in diameter. It is important that you do not step out of this circle until the ritual is over. This is because all of the power and energy will be contained inside the circle.

The circle can be marked in a number of ways. If the floor is linoleum, you might want to draw a circle in white chalk on it. This can easily be removed afterwards. Alternatively, you might use wool, thread, string, rope or masking tape to make an impromptu circle. No matter which method you select, ensure that the circle is white in color. Many people find that drawing a circle is a complicated business. An excellent remedy is to paint a circle onto a large sheet of plastic or oilcloth. This can be placed on the floor whenever necessary, and folded up and put away when not in use. Friends of mine have a large, circular rug that they use.

You will need two white candles. These should be placed on either side of your altar. You do not need new candles every time you conduct a ritual. However, you need to ensure that there is enough burning time left in them to last until the end of the ritual.

You will also need incense. This serves a number of purposes. It effectively purifies the room. It helps create the right vibrations for magic to occur. In many of the older religions, it was believed that incense carried prayers directly to the gods.

Any incense will do. I tend to avoid incense sticks, but they can be useful if you do not have much time or if you do not have a censer (incense burner). Frankincense is my personal favorite, as the scent brings back many almost forgotten memories. Choose something that appeals to you.

Finally, you will need your pendulum. This should be placed in the center of your altar.

Preparation

Take a shower or bath before conducting the ritual. Think of the questions you are going to ask. If there are many of these you might want to write them down.

The Ritual

The first stage of the ritual is the Opening. Stand outside the circle and ask for peace and protection. You ask this of whichever deity you wish. If you were brought up in the Judeo-Christian tradition, you will probably call on your spirit guides, archangels or angel guardians. However, you may prefer to call on Horus, Apollo, Arthur, Gaia, Frigga, Minerva, or any other god or goddess that you choose.

The exact words you use for the Opening are up to you. You might say something like this:

> "I ask for peace, love and protection. When I enter the circle, I request the aid of my guides to help me achieve my goals, which are for the benefit of everyone involved. I also ask Raphael, Michael, Gabriel, and Uriel for help, guidance and protection. Please protect me and surround me with energy and divine love. Thank you."

Enter the circle and stand facing the altar. Pause for a minute or two. Imagine yourself surrounded by a circle of protection, and feel the special energies as you stand inside it.

Light the left candle, followed by the right. Pick up the censer and, holding it high, walk around the inside of the circle in a clockwise direction. You should walk around the circle three times, and finally stop facing the altar again. You will probably find it helpful to imagine that you are walking in a spiral as you do this. Place the censer back on the altar.

Pick up your pendulum and rest it in your left palm. Cover this palm with your right hand, and raise both hands to shoulder height. Say the following words (or something similar that feels right for you):

"I ask for thy blessing on my pendulum. I pray that you allow it to give true and honest answers to the questions I am going to ask. Please protect my pendulum, and imbue it with universal love."

Pause for thirty seconds, and then say, "thank you."

Now it is time to start using the pendulum to obtain answers to your questions. Start with the least important questions. If you have a large number of questions, write down the answers the pendulum gives as you receive them.

Once you have finished asking questions, place the pendulum down on the altar.

It is now time to thank the four archangels for their assistance and protection. You should pause and visualize the archangels in your mind, before speaking the words of thanks. It is important not to hurry this part of the ritual.

Hold your arms out to the east and say:

"Thank you, Raphael, for your protection and strength. Thank you for allowing me to perform this rite of divination, and thank you for the answers it has provided."

Turn to the south, extend your arms, and say:

"Thank you, Michael, for your protection and strength. Thank you for allowing me to perform this rite of divination, and thank you for the answers it has provided."

Turn to the west, extend your arms, and say:

"Thank you, Gabriel, for your protection and strength. Thank you for allowing me to perform this rite of divination, and thank you for the answers it has provided."

Turn to the north, extend your arms, and say:

"Thank you, Uriel, for your protection and strength. Thank you for allowing me to perform this rite of divination, and thank you for the answers it has provided."

Turn to the east again and extinguish the candles and the censer. Pause in front of the altar for two or three minutes and give silent thanks. Allow yourself to become mentally prepared for your normal everyday life before leaving the protection of the circle.

A ritual opens up your psychic centers. Because of this, many people find it hard to return to everyday life after performing a ritual. I have got into the habit of clapping my hands above my head as soon as I leave the magic circle. You may find that this is helpful for you, too. Alternatively, find something else to do as soon as you leave the protection of the circle. Snapping your fingers, stamping your feet, jumping up and down, whistling, and stretching are all good ways of letting go of the energies that have been created in the course of the ritual.

This simple ritual helps to awaken your magic perceptions. The seriousness and deliberation of it give the divination ritual enormous power for good. This ritual also gives your pendulum unbelievable energy. You should be able to sense this in your pendulum hours, and sometimes even days, after the ritual.

Incidentally, once your pendulum has been blessed in this ritual, it should never be used for flippant or frivolous purposes. You may like to use a special pendulum that is used only when you are performing this ritual.

There is a danger in rituals that I should mention. When you rely on a ritual to reach a certain state of being, there is a tendency to lean more and more on the ritual itself. Ultimately, you are likely to believe that it is the ritual that is doing the magic, rather than the pendulum, or, ultimately, you.

A friend of mine always uses the same music when he meditates. He is now convinced that it would be impossible for him to meditate to any other music, because, in his mind, he thinks that it is the music that creates the meditative state. The music has become a crutch that he leans on.

Do not let this happen with you. Change the ritual whenever you feel like it, even in the middle if it seems right. There is no need to use formal or involved patterns of speech. Experiment. Speak from your heart. The best results come when you perform the ritual in an open, innocent, trusting manner. Do not let your rituals become staid, formal procedures that you act out like an automaton.

chapter nine

Self-Improvement with the Pendulum

Your pendulum can become a powerful tool to guide you in making the correct decisions on all matters in your life. You will find, as an additional benefit, that your pendulum is also therapeutic. Many people experience a sense of peace and calm when they use their pendulums on a regular basis.[1]

Suppose you are looking for a new job, one that is much better than your current job. You see an intriguing advertisement in the newspaper. The position sounds exciting, but is it the right career move for you?

The best thing to do is to ask your pendulum before applying for the job. You should ask if you would enjoy the new job. Would it be too stressful? Would you find it easy to get along with your new colleagues? Would you be able to handle the commute? Would a change at this time be beneficial to your career in the long term? Would this career move be good for your family?

By doing this, your pendulum will save you from wasting time applying for positions that are not suitable for you. You can also use the pendulum when you apply for the position. Ask the pendulum if your résumé and letter of application are good enough to attract attention. The pendulum will tell you what needs to be done to make these selling tools as powerful as possible.

You should also ask the pendulum questions after the job interview. Would the position be challenging enough for you? Would you enjoy working in that particular environment? Is the corporation reputable? Do you really want this particular job?

You can follow the same process with every area of your life. Should you ask a certain person out? Should you join this club? Should you stay at home this vacation? Much of the time your pendulum will confirm what you already know. However, at times, the answers you are given will surprise you.

Martin, a young friend of mine, had just completed a liberal arts degree at college. He was not sure what career he wanted to pursue. His plan was to continue at college and get his Master's degree. It sounded like a good, logical move as he had no other clear ideas about his future. When he asked his pendulum about it, the response was that he should not continue with this course of study. Martin was so surprised at this that it was several days before he asked his pendulum any more questions.

During this time he gave a great deal of thought to his future, and knew what questions to ask his pendulum. The pendulum suggested that he take a year off to travel. This sounded like an impossible dream, but Martin found that with his qualifications he could get a job teaching English to students in Japan. After a year in Japan, he returned home and was offered a good position with a corporation that imported goods from Japan and distributed them throughout North America.

"If you'd told me five years ago that this was what I'd be doing, I'd have laughed," he told me. "But my pendulum knew. I was planning to stay in college only because I didn't know what else to do."

Deep down, Martin knew that carrying on in college was not the right thing for him to do, but he was not prepared to admit it, even to himself, until his pendulum told him so.

Another friend of mine has twice enrolled for college courses that he did not complete. Even before he started the courses he knew that they were not right for him, but he tried to deny these feelings, and consequently wasted a great deal of time and money. If he had asked his pendulum before enrolling for the courses, he would not have taken them.

Frequently, we set goals to please others, rather than ourselves. Goals of this sort are only ever achieved at enormous cost, and the failure rate is high. This creates a loss of self-esteem and feelings of uselessness.

Obviously, we have a much greater chance of success in reaching any goal if we desire it greatly. As the pendulum gives us access to our inner mind, it can tell us whether or not we really desire a certain goal, and are prepared to pay whatever price is necessary. If we do not desire a certain goal, it probably will not happen.

Many years ago I spent time with a swimming coach. He told me that he knew virtually right away which of his students would become successful. "They have a certain spark or attitude," he told me. "They are determined to win and are prepared to do anything necessary to make it happen. They'll pay the price." In other words, they have a strong desire and will do whatever is necessary to make it happen.

Fortunately, we can use the pendulum to help us choose goals that are right for us. My former dentist always hated his occupation and wanted to be a photographer. However, with a wife, family, and mortgage, he found it too difficult to change career and spent forty years doing something he detested. If he had consulted a pendulum before starting to study dentistry, his whole life would have been totally different. It would certainly have been much more fulfilling and happier. As it was, he had to work extremely hard every day, as he hated what he was doing. No matter how much money he made, it was drudgery. If he had become a photographer, he would have worked just as hard, but it would have seemed like play, because he would have been doing what he really wanted to do.

Mental Development

Life is a learning process, and we should regard education as a lifelong process. Our brains have an unlimited potential. There is no risk of filling our brains with too much information. There are also numerous opportunities to learn and grow. Reading is a good example. There are many courses available on any subject you could care to name.

If you are not sure what books to read or what courses to take, ask your pendulum. You might be surprised at the answers. I have read many books that I would have overlooked without the advice of my pendulum.

I do not usually use my pendulum in bookstores. If I am not certain which book to buy, or whether or not to buy a certain book, I use my entire body as a type of pendulum. I close my eyes and silently ask if I should buy the book I am thinking about. If my body feels drawn toward the book, I will buy it. If I feel no response, or am actually repelled, I will leave the book on the shelves.

There have been occasions when I have wanted to buy two books, but only had enough money on me to buy one. In this case, I place the two books a couple of feet apart, close my eyes, and ask which book I should buy today. My body will be drawn toward the book that would be most useful to me immediately.

This is a form of body dowsing.[2] You can use your body in this way any time you have to make a decision, but do not have a pendulum with you, or do not want to attract attention to yourself by using it in public.

Physical Development

Some years ago, my younger son decided to join a gym. There were several to choose from, and he felt totally confused after visiting all of them. As I was paying for his gym membership, he was not particularly concerned about the costs involved, and was thinking about joining the most expensive one. I suggested that we put the question of gym membership to the pendulum.

We asked the pendulum to rate the gyms in terms of the benefits Philip was hoping to achieve. To our surprise, we found that the gym that was second to cheapest appeared to be the best gym for him to join. Philip took out a one-month membership to see what it was like. Today, some years later, he still belongs to the same gym.

You can ask your pendulum a variety of questions about your physical fitness. I was a keen jogger until I reached my mid-thirties. At that stage I began having problems with my knees. My pendulum suggested that I give up jogging and find another method of exercise. If I had not asked these questions, I might have continued jogging until I did major damage to my knees.

You can also ask your pendulum questions about the health benefits of the exercise you are doing. A friend of mine was surprised to learn that he was not gaining the health benefits he thought he was from his weekly game of golf. According to his pendulum, golf, and particularly the way he played it, was a leisure activity, rather than a sport. His pendulum suggested that skipping was the best form of exercise for him. My friend took up skipping and is physically in much better shape than he has been in for many years.

Emotional Development

Your emotions can be hard to control at times. Some people seem to do an effective job at bottling their emotions up, but they seem to pay a high price for it. Other people appear to express their emotions freely everywhere they go.

Naturally, there are times when you want to express your emotions and other times when you would prefer to keep them hidden.

You can ask your pendulum to help you find appropriate responses.

Spiritual Development

Your pendulum can even help you to develop spiritually. Today many people are searching for a faith, something to believe in. You can ask your pendulum questions about different churches, different faiths, and different religions.

You are a spiritual being. Spirituality is an expression of the creative spirit of your soul. It is a useful experiment to hold your pendulum and say the following words:

> "I am divine love. I am universal love. I am a spiritual being. I am."

The pendulum should react to this by giving you a positive response. If your pendulum fails to react, or reacts negatively, say the words several times a day as an affirmation.

After a few days, say the words while holding your pendulum. Keep on doing this until you do receive a positive response.

Self-Assessment

Your pendulum enables you to explore your subconscious mind. This is a revealing exercise, and you may not be happy with all of the answers you receive. However, it is important, because it enables you to assess yourself and start working on making changes to any aspect of your personality that you are not happy with.

All you need is your pendulum and a quiet place where you will not be interrupted. Sit down comfortably and say the following statements out loud. Pause after saying each one, and see what your pendulum is doing. It will move in a positive direction if your subconscious mind agrees with what you have said. It will not do anything if it is unsure of the answer, or has no strong views on the statement. Finally, it will give a negative response if it disagrees with the statement.

Record your answers and repeat this exercise regularly. This gives you feedback on how you have progressed in the interim.

Here are the statements:

I am happy.

I am loved.

I am a good person.

I am successful.

I am following my heart's desire.

I deserve to be successful.

I deserve all the good things life has to offer.

I enjoy excellent health.

I am positive.

I am enthusiastic.

I am confident.

I achieve my goals.

I attract good things to me.

I am free from stress.

You can add any other statements that you wish. If you are married, you might say: "My marriage is a happy one." Naturally, you would not say that if you were single. Choose statements that relate to what is going on in your life. Try not to think of the responses as you do the exercise. Record them and immediately move on to the next statement.

Once you have completed this, look at the statements that received a negative response. You may, or may not, know why the pendulum gave this answer. If you are tentative and unsure of yourself, you may not be surprised if the pendulum denied that you were confident. However, you may have thought that you were perfectly happy and been surprised at the negative response your pendulum gave.

You can ask your pendulum a series of questions to determine why it gave the responses it did. Once you know the underlying reasons, you can take action to remedy the situation.

It does you good to pause every now and again to assess yourself. Most people get caught up in the hustle and bustle of everyday life and do not make time to assess themselves and monitor their progress.

Affirmation Experiment

Here is another experiment that can be highly revealing.

Sit down comfortably somewhere, and say the following statement out loud:

> "Everything is going well for me. I am successful, prosperous, and happy."

Many people find it difficult to say those words. They don't feel as if everything is going well for them. They certainly don't feel successful, prosperous or even particularly happy. Think about the words and what they mean. Your subconscious mind accepts, and acts upon, the suggestions given to it. When you say: "Everything is going well for me," your subconscious mind is not going to argue. Your conscious mind might disagree, but your subconscious mind accepts good thoughts that are presented to it. It then acts on them, and makes them happen. Consequently, if you say: "Everything is going well for me" often enough for the thought to become lodged deeply into your subconscious mind, it will become a fact in your life.

The same thing applies to the second sentence: "I am successful, prosperous, and happy." These statements mean different things to different people. If you are doing what you love to do, and are heading towards some worthwhile goals, I would say you were "successful, prosperous, and happy." I would not be able to say that if you were a multi-millionaire, with no goals, no real friends and nothing to live for.

Say the affirmation again:

> "Everything is going well for me. I am successful, prosperous, and happy."

Say it with feeling, and imagine the affirmation reaching your subconscious mind and finding a welcome home there.

Finally, hold your pendulum and say the affirmation ten times. Emphasize different words each time you say it.

Once you have done this, look at your pendulum. It should be moving in your positive direction. Become aware of your body, and feel the sense of surety inside yourself, telling you that everything is going well for you, and that you are unbelievably successful, prosperous, and happy.

Changing Programmed Behavior Patterns

We all have bad habits of various sorts. Every now and again, often as a New Year resolution, we try to eliminate them. Have you ever said: "This year I'm going to stop smoking," or "I'm going to lose thirty pounds"? Often this is just wishful thinking, of course, but sometimes we really mean it. We intend to lose that weight or eliminate that bad habit, but try as we might, it never happens.

The reason this occurs is that we are trying to change well-entrenched patterns of behavior using the force of our will. This very seldom works.

Fortunately, we can use our pendulum to determine what the deeply entrenched feelings are, and then reprogram ourselves to eliminate the old patterns and replace them with new ones.

Let's use losing weight as an example.

Losing Weight

In my work as a hypnotherapist, I have helped many people to lose weight over the years. I also created Perma-Loss, a permanent weight control program that was marketed in several countries by infomercials.[3] Consequently, I have more than twenty-five years of experience in this field.

In my private sessions, I frequently asked my clients to use a pendulum. Once they become used to it, and determined the different responses, I have them say the following statements while holding the pendulum.

> *I weigh "xyz" pounds.* (This is the person's current weight. The pendulum should provide a positive response to this.)

> *I will be much happier when I lose weight.* (People expect a positive response to this question. If the answer is negative, more questions need to be asked to clarify this.)

In three months time I will weigh "abc" pounds. (A positive response indicates that your subconscious mind will allow you to lose the desired amount of weight. A negative response occurs more frequently than a positive one.)

I want to weigh "abc" pounds because . . . [I will look better, feel better, be healthier, be able to buy clothes on sale, etc.] (Watch the pendulum to see what response it gives to all of your reasons for wanting to lose weight.)

Will you help me achieve this goal? My goal is to weigh "abc" pounds in three months. (If the answer to this is positive, you can start asking the pendulum which forms of exercise would be best for you, what food you should eat and avoid, and so on. Every day, suspend your pendulum and say: "I am going to weigh 'abc' pounds in three months." The pendulum should react positively to this every day.)

The weight will come off effortlessly when you have your subconscious mind working with you, rather than fighting you every inch of the way.

If the pendulum refuses to help you, you must find out why. People have a huge variety of reasons for putting on weight. Some of the reasons make no sense logically, but they are accepted and acted upon by the subconscious mind.

One woman I saw years ago had been badly hurt by someone she loved. Her subconscious mind decided to protect her and she put on weight to make herself unattractive to men. The extra weight was a form of protection. This was not done consciously. Consciously, she wanted to meet the right man and settle down, but her subconscious mind was actively working against this goal. Once she discovered the reasons why she had put on so much weight, and discussed with her subconscious mind, via the pendulum, why she wanted to become slim again, the weight began to come off.

Poverty Consciousness

Negative feelings about money are common, and usually date back to childhood. Money is essential if you want to live a comfortable and pleasant life. There is nothing intrinsically bad about money. However, the attitudes that many people have about it are wrong. People tend to be ruled by money. In fact, money should be our servant.

If you are not happy with your current financial situation, say the following statements while holding your pendulum and see what responses you get.

I like money.

I deserve to be rich.

I have a positive cash flow.

I have all the money I need.

I always have everything I need.

My income is (whatever your current income is at the time you do this experiment).

I would be happy with an annual income of . . . (Be outrageous here. At the very least, double your current income. If you receive a negative response, drop the proposed income by ten percent. Keep on doing this until your pendulum gives you a positive reading.)

I am prepared to do whatever is necessary to earn this amount of money. (This is the amount that the pendulum gave a positive response to.)

Money is my friend.

I enjoy spending money.

Good things come to me without effort.

The results of this test can be extremely revealing. You may discover feelings and attitudes about money that you were not aware you had. Fortunately, as I am sure you know by now, you can change any negative perceptions about money that you currently have, and replace them with positive feelings.

Irwin, a friend of mine, is a self-employed entertainer. For several years, he earned roughly the same amount of money each year. One year it would be up a few thousand, and the following year it would be down slightly. He complained to me that there seemed to be a barrier that stopped him moving ahead financially.

When we asked the pendulum questions about this, it emerged that his father had always had a safe, secure job and was opposed to Irwin making a living in what he thought was a highly risky field. His father was extremely conservative financially, and Irwin had subconsciously absorbed these views about money. Consequently, although he was self-employed in a field with potentially unlimited scope for financial progress, he had become stuck earning a modest income similar to that of his father.

After expenses, Irwin was making about forty thousand a year. He told me that he wanted to make one hundred thousand dollars in a single year, as no one in his family had ever had such a large income. Irwin sat down with his pendulum and said, "I am comfortable making one hundred thousand dollars a year." The pendulum gave a negative response.

This was not surprising, given Irwin's previous financial history. I suggested he do two things:

1. He should repeat the words: "I am comfortable making one hundred thousand dollars a year," as many times as possible every day. In other words, he was to use it as an affirmation.

2. He should say the same words out loud at least once every day while holding his pendulum.

An interesting thing happened. The pendulum gave a negative response for six days, and then started saying that it did not want to answer. On the tenth day, the pendulum began giving a positive response. I knew then that Irwin would finally move ahead financially.

Once his subconscious mind accepted the fact that Irwin could, and should, make a six-figure income, it began working on it. Several opportunities came his way, and the money started rolling in. Less than a year later, Irwin had revised his income figure up to one hundred and twenty thousand.

Gambling, Smoking, and Other Addictions

You can use the same process to eliminate all sorts of negative traits and habits that you are not happy with. Gambling and smoking are two that I see frequently.

Use the pendulum to determine your innermost feelings about the problem. Visualize yourself in the near future, enjoying life free of the problem that has been holding you back. Ask your pendulum if it will help you become free of the problem. Keep on doing this every day until your pendulum agrees. Create an affirmation, such as: "I am free of the nicotine habit. I am a nonsmoker." Repeat this as frequently as possible every day, and say it at least once a day while holding your pendulum. You will find that once your subconscious mind is happy with your decision, the process of change will be put into place automatically, and you will achieve your goal.

chapter ten

The Pendulum in Home & Garden

YOUR PENDULUM CAN be a useful tool in your home environment to ensure that it is perfect for you and your needs. If you are looking for a home to buy or rent, you can ask your pendulum about each place you visit. It may see possibilities in places that you would be inclined to overlook.

You can also save a great deal of time by asking your pendulum about different localities. Ask if you would be happy in each place. Given a choice of a number of locations, it will tell you which one would be the most beneficial for you and your family.

Once you have found a suitable home, stand at the entrance of the property with your pendulum in your hand. If you are moving into a house with a garden, your property starts at the main gate. If you are moving into an apartment building, your property begins at the entrance to your apartment. Your pendulum should start to revolve. Once it starts moving, slowly walk through the house as if you were taking a friend on a tour of your new home. Whenever possible, leave each room by a different entrance to the one you came in by. Your pendulum should continue to revolve in a circular direction throughout this inspection. This is the ideal scenario.

However, it may stop or change direction. This is an indication of stagnant ch'i energy.[1] Ch'i is the universal life force, and we want as much of it as possible inside our home. Feng shui is the ancient Chinese art of living in harmony with the world. In feng shui we want the beneficial ch'i to enter through the main entrance and flow smoothly throughout the house. This blockage of energy could be caused by a number of factors. Clutter is a major one. Obviously, the remedy is to remove it. Straight lines and sharp angles cause shars, or negative energy. The remedy is to remove the offending object, or to deflect it back where it came from. This can be done with additional lighting or a mirror. Once you have made changes, walk through the house again with your pendulum and see what it has to tell you. You may have to rearrange furniture, or perhaps add some potted plants to create more beneficial ch'i.

Once you are established in your home, you can continue to fine-tune your environment to make it as ideal as possible.

You might decide to do some home decorating. Ask your pendulum about the different color schemes you have in mind. It will tell you which combinations would be best for you and your needs. You can choose carpets, rugs, and furniture in the same way.

We all spend about a third of our lives in bed. The position of the bed is extremely important to our health and well-being. You can use your pendulum to determine the best placement of your bed. Changing the position of the bed has helped many insomniacs enjoy a good night's sleep.[2]

You can test your own bed in two ways. One is to simply ask the pendulum questions about your bed. Ask if the bed is in the right place. If the pendulum gives a negative answer, continue to ask questions until you determine where the bed should be.

The other method is to stand beside the bed, with your free hand between the bed and the pendulum. The free hand should be held a couple of inches above the surface of the bed, and the pendulum should be held a couple of inches over the free hand. Your bed is considered to be in a good position if the pendulum rotates, and in a bad location if the pendulum swings.

You can also suspend your pendulum over the different colors in paint charts to determine the best colors in which to redecorate your home. Again, ask your pendulum if you would be happy living with this color in your home. Once you have narrowed the choice down, determine which color would be the most beneficial for you.

In the Garden

Most people have heard of Cleve Backster's experiments with plants. Cleve is an expert on lie detection. In 1966, he attached a polygraph to a philodendron in his office, and discovered that it gave an emotional response. Knowing that the responses on a polygraph test are most marked when the person feels threatened, Cleve mused to himself about burning the plant. The instant he thought about this, the pen recorder jumped. Somehow, the plant had picked up Cleve Backster's thoughts and reacted. After this almost accidental start, scientists started looking at the subject seriously. They eventually proved that plants respond to what is going on around them.[3] They respond positively to good thoughts, and negatively to bad thoughts. Consequently, it pays to think positive thoughts while tending to your plants. It also shows the enormous benefits that can be gained by talking to your plants.

Your pendulum can help you to communicate with your plants. It can also be used in many other ways to help you become a better gardener. For instance, let's assume that you have just bought a new plant, shrub, or perhaps a packet of seeds. You can ask your pendulum if you should plant it immediately. If you get a negative response, ask if you should plant it in a week's time, and continue asking questions until it gives a positive response. You can then ask where the plant should be placed in your garden. You probably have a place in mind, but your pendulum might have other ideas. Once you have chosen a suitable site for your new purchase, but before planting it, ask questions about the soil. Is there sufficient drainage? Is more compost required? What fertilizer would the plant like? Finally, ask what size hole should be dug.

Your pendulum can give advice on what nutrients are best for certain plants. You might ask a plant if it is receiving enough sunlight. Your pendulum can tell you if you are giving your plants enough water. You should ask your potted plants every now and again if they need repotting. It can also advise you on the best places to plant new plants. You can also determine the quality of different supplements you might be tempted to buy. Given a choice of fertilizers, your pendulum will tell you which one would be best for you and your needs.

If a potted plant ceases to thrive, you can ask your pendulum if it is pot-bound. If so, you can repot it in a larger container. If the potted plant is indoors, it may need to be placed in a different location. Your pendulum will be able to determine this for you.

You can suspend your pendulum over any plant, indoors or out, and ask about its well-being. You might ask if it needs more or less water. Does it need more nourishment? Does it have all the nutrients that it needs? How about trace elements? Would it be happier if moved to a different location? Would it like you to talk to it more often? Is it ready for pruning? There is no limit to the questions that can be asked.

One woman I know dances and sings to her plants for twenty minutes every morning. The plants in her conservatory have thrived ever since she started doing this. She used her pendulum to find out how she could look after her plants better. Much to her surprise, they told her that they wanted her to sing and dance.

"I can't cheat and play CDs," she told me. "My plants know. Heaven knows, I'm not much of a singer, or a dancer, for that matter, but my plants seem to thrive on it. And it gives me a fantastic start to the day, too!"

If the plant is too large for you to suspend the pendulum over it, you can stand beside it and use your pendulum there. A friend of mine began doing this with a large grove of trees in a park near her home. She found that once she had made friends with the trees, she no longer needed to use her pendulum. She and her trees communicate with each other telepathically, and she is constantly aware of their health and well-being.

In the course of her work, she accidentally found what she calls the "spiritual center" of each tree. While holding her pendulum, she slowly walks around each tree until the pendulum stops moving. This is the spiritual center. She talks to the spiritual centers of each of her trees, and is ecstatic about the results.

She believes that when she speaks directly to the plant's spiritual center growth is encouraged. She also feels that if the right crystal is placed at the spiritual center the results would be incredible. She is still researching this, and plans to eventually write a book on the subject.

Native Americans would absorb energy from certain trees by standing with their backs pressed against their trunks. It would be interesting to know if they were pressing against the spiritual center of these trees. It is said that the German Chancellor Otto von Bismarck (1815–1898) stood against an oak tree for half an hour every day.[4]

Some years ago, Adele, a woman I know, was given a bunch of roses by a friend. There is nothing unusual about this, except for maybe one thing. Her friend selected the flowers using a pendulum. The friend knew that certain flowers contain healing properties, and carefully chose these specific roses to help Adele cope in a difficult time.

Interestingly, there is a scientific basis for this. Dr. Nikolai Yurchenko, a Russian scientist, spent more than twenty years studying the influence plants have on human health. He found that certain plants, such as willows, birches, oaks, and roses, possess healing qualities.[5] Adele's friend had heard of this research and asked his pendulum to choose flowers that would be beneficial for her. As well as giving Adele a welcome and beautiful surprise gift, he also sent her a present that would help her become whole again.

It's hard to think of a better use for the humble pendulum.

chapter eleven

Real Magic with the Pendulum

YOU HAVE LEARNED how to use the pendulum for a variety of important needs, such as finding a lost object, ensuring good health, protection, and self-improvement. This is information that can transform your life. Now we are going to take it a step further and learn how to influence the future to make your life exactly what you want it to be.

Up until now, we have been accessing our subconscious minds to achieve our goals. Now we are going to learn how to consciously influence our subconscious minds to make our desires a reality.

Nothing can happen without desire. Desire means you will be prepared to do whatever is necessary to achieve your goal. If you would like something, but do not desire it with a passion, it is unlikely that you will achieve it.

It can be a useful exercise to sit down somewhere where you will not be disturbed, and make a list of all the things you would like to have in your life. Here are some suggestions to get you started:

A warm, loving relationship.

A comfortable home.

An overseas vacation.

Vibrant health.

Further education.

A well-paid, interesting job.

A close family life.

Money in the bank (state exact amount desired).

You will find that your desires will most likely fall into just a few categories: career, education, health, love, money, and travel.

It does not matter what you write down, as no one will see your list unless you show it to others. Carry your list with you for a few days, so that you can add items as they occur to you.

When you feel ready, sit down quietly again and write each item down on a separate piece of paper. Go through the sheets of paper and arrange them in order of desire. The item you desire the most should be on top.

Place the first piece of paper in front of you and suspend your pendulum over it. Think about this desire and how achieving it would change your life. Think about what your life would be like once you have this particular goal.

Watch what your pendulum is doing. If it is moving in a positive direction, it is an indication that you feel inwardly comfortable with that particular goal. Conversely, if your pendulum is reacting negatively it means that you are not inwardly comfortable with your goal.

In this case you will have to start asking your pendulum questions. Do I really want this goal? Am I prepared to do whatever is necessary to achieve it? Will I be happier than I am now once this goal is achieved?

You may find that something you thought you wanted desperately is not that important to you after all. You may find that you are perfectly satisfied with your life as it is, and are not prepared to do the things that are required to achieve this goal. Perhaps the desire for it is not really there, after all.

Stuart is a thirty-three-year-old high school teacher. He loves his work, but gave it up for a short time a few years ago. He decided that he could make more money cleaning windows than he could teaching school. He found that this was the case, but he hated every minute he spent cleaning windows. He discovered that his goal was not money after all. He is now much more contented as a teacher than he ever was before.

Use your pendulum over each piece of paper in turn. Make notes of the responses you get from each one. You might want to place the sheets of paper into three piles: one in which the pendulum gave a positive response, another in which it gave a negative response, and a third pile for the desires that your pendulum either did not answer, or gave an "I don't know" or "I don't want to answer."

Keep all of the papers and repeat this exercise two or three times over the next week. One or two goals from the third pile might need to be placed in the first pile. It is unlikely that any goals from the first or second piles will need to be changed, but it does sometimes happen.

At the end of the week, place all the goals from the first pile in a row in front of you. Use your pendulum to confirm that you do really want these goals, and that you are prepared to do whatever is necessary to achieve them. Then use your pendulum to decide which goal you will work on first.

There is no reason why you should not work on two or three goals at the same time, but you need one specific goal to focus on. Hopefully, among these desires is one goal that you have a burning desire to achieve.

Once your pendulum has chosen a goal for you, put the other desires aside. Select a word or short phrase to represent the goal you will be focusing on, and write this down on a small piece of card, small enough to carry with you at all times. This phrase needs to be written in the present tense, as if you have already achieved it. If, for example, you want to be vice president of the company you work for, you should write: "I am vice president of XYZ Corporation." Your subconscious mind does not know if what you are saying is true or not, but it will work on making it a reality in your life.

You may wish to carry a photograph or drawing of your goal instead of words on paper. A picture of your desire is an extremely effective way of attracting to you what you want. Conrad Hilton, founder of the prestigious Hilton Hotels chain, carried a picture of the Waldorf-Astoria Hotel in his pocket for almost twenty-five years before he finally managed to buy it. Carrying the picture constantly reinforced his desire to one day own that hotel.

It is important that you look at this card several times every day. If you carry it in your purse or wallet you will be automatically reminded of your goal every time you see it. Advertisers know the power of repetition. You will learn it too, as you practice this exercise.

At least once a day, suspend your pendulum over this piece of card and speak your desire out loud. The pendulum should give a positive response every time you do this. As it does this say aloud, with as much enthusiasm as you can, "Yes, yes, yes!"

You are doing a number of different things here. The word or phrase you have written down is an affirmation. There is enormous power in affirmations and repeating them over and over again implants them more and more deeply into your subconscious mind. Every time you read your affirmation reinforces this. Say your affirmation out loud whenever possible, so that you can hear the affirmation, as well as looking at it or reading it.

The pendulum is extremely important in this process. The positive movements it makes are produced by your subconscious mind. It shows that your subconscious, inner mind is happy about what you are doing and will help you make it a reality.

When you say the words "yes, yes, yes," you add energy to your desire. This tells your subconscious mind how motivated and enthusiastic you are about reaching this goal.

Finally, during the few minutes it takes to perform this exercise you will be totally focused on your goal. Once the exercise has been completed, you can let go of your goal and carry on with your day, confident that your subconscious mind will be working on making it a reality, even though you are busy doing other things.

With all of this happening every single day, your subconscious mind will work hard to make your desire a reality. You may have no idea how it will happen, but your subconscious mind will work on it and find a way.

Be receptive to any ideas that occur to you. They will be messages from your subconscious mind. Write them down so they are not forgotten. Act on them.

Repeat this exercise with your pendulum at least once every day until your desire has materialized. Anything worthwhile takes time and effort. Be patient, and enjoy the journey.

chapter twelve

Advanced Pendulum Magic

YOU WILL NOW learn how to accomplish what could be considered miracles with the pendulum. Before doing that, though, here is some background into an area of Hawaiian spirituality known as Huna.

Huna magic is incredibly powerful, as long as it is performed correctly. I know many people who have achieved wonderful things with Huna. I also know people who have not been successful with it. This is because they were not doing it correctly. By using your pendulum, along with Huna principles, you can be sure to do everything correctly at each stage.

The Story of Huna

Back in the 1970s I was given a small book called *Introduction to Huna* by Max Freedom Long.[1] It took me several months to get around to reading it, but once I started, I was hooked. I immediately bought all of Max Freedom Long's other books, and as many other books on the subject as possible. What particularly excited me was that the Kahunas had created a simple, workable, and completely logical system for living in harmony with the Earth and for achieving their goals. In all the years since, I have found nothing to equal the beauty and practicality of this system.

Yet it was almost lost forever.

In 1917, Max Freedom Long was a young schoolteacher on the Big Island of Hawaii. He spent a great deal of time with the native people and enjoyed listening to their stories. Every now and again, in these conversations, reference was made to the Kahunas, but when Max asked questions about them, no one was willing to answer.[2]

Max became fascinated with the stories. Was it really possible for the Kahunas to perform instantaneous healings and to walk barefooted on hot lava? Although the local people were not prepared to tell him, as an outsider, anything about the Kahunas, Max was able to read about them. He learned that the Kahunas had been outlawed since the days of the early Christian missionaries. Although they still existed, everything they did was in secret.

After three years on the Big Island, Max went to Oahu and visited William Tufts Brigham, the curator of the Bishop Museum in Honolulu. Dr. Brigham had spent most of his life studying anything to do with Hawaii, and Max hoped that he might receive honest and serious answers to his questions.

He was expecting to be disappointed yet again, but Dr. Brigham was excited to meet him. He was eighty-two-years old, and was thrilled to find someone who was keen to carry on researching the mysterious beliefs and practices of the Kahuna.

Max studied with Dr. Brigham for four years until the old man died. Max stayed in Hawaii for a further five years, struggling both to support himself and to learn the secrets of the Kahunas. In 1931 he was forced to give up. He returned to California where he ran a camera shop. He remained fascinated with the Kahunas, but had to put it to one side while he concentrated on running a business.

In 1935, in the early hours of the morning, he woke up with the idea that helped him to finally unlock the hidden secrets he had been searching for for so long. He realized that the Kahunas had to have names for the different parts of their magic. He began studying the root words of the Hawaiian language.

Dr. Brigham had taught him three important things to look for:

1. There had to be a consciousness directing the process of magic.
2. There had to be some type of force.
3. There had to be some type of substance through which the force could act.

It took Max less than a year to identify the first two, but it was another six years before he found the last one.

His first book on the subject was published in England in 1936.[3] Max dedicated the rest of his life to exploring, researching, and promoting Huna. He founded Huna Research Associates in 1945. His major book *The Secret Science Behind Miracles* was published in 1948, and has been continuously in print ever since. Max died in 1971, a month before his eighty-first birthday. At the time of his death he was still actively involved in the work of Huna Research Associates.

What is Huna?

Huna is a Hawaiian word meaning "secret." It is the name that Max Freedom Long gave to the practical system of psychology he discovered after many years of research. Huna describes the psycho-religious methods practiced by the Hawaiian Kahunas to create magic and, sometimes, miracles.

No one knows where it came from originally, although there are many hypotheses. The most accepted story is that the secrets originally came from twelve tribes of people who lived thousands of years ago in the area the Sahara desert occupies today. As their fertile land gradually turned into desert, the tribes headed east and spent time building the Great Pyramid in Egypt. They were probably also involved in the mystery schools of that period.

These people saw difficult times ahead and wanted to preserve their secrets. In clairvoyant dreams they saw uninhabited islands in the Pacific Ocean where they would be able to practice their beliefs in perfect safety. One tribe decided to stay in northern Africa, but the others travelled across Asia to Hawaii.

One of the readers of Max Freedom Long's first book was a retired journalist named Reginald Stewart. As a young man he had been taught magic by a primitive Berber tribe in the Atlas Mountains of North Africa. He instantly realized that the beliefs and practices of the Kahunas must have come from the same original source that the Berbers had used. Many of the words they used were identical.[4]

Huna Beliefs

The basic concept of Huna is that we are comprised of three minds, or selves, in one. Max Freedom Long called these the low, middle, and high selves. The Kahunas called them *unihipili* (low self), *uhane* (middle self), and *aumakua* (high self). These relate to the terms subconscious, conscious, and superconscious that are used in modern psychology.

In fact, the system that the Kahunas devised thousands of years ago is more sophisticated and complete than anything psychologists have managed to devise. The psychology of the Kahunas shows people how to achieve their goals, and also explains why many people fail to reach them.

These three selves are actually all aspects of our mind. However, the Kahunas visualized them as being in different parts of the body. The low self was situated in the solar plexus. The middle self was in the left side of the head, and the high self was situated above the head.

When the three selves work in harmony with each other there is no limit to what a person can achieve. If one of the selves is out of balance with the others, illnesses and other problems can occur.

The Middle Self (Thinking Self)

We will start with the middle self as this relates to our conscious mind. This is where we think and make decisions. It is logical, analytical, and goal-setting. It is the thinking part of our being and is what most people think of when they refer to themselves. Although we experience the middle self in our heads, its influence can be felt in every part of the body.

The Low Self (Feeling Self)

The low self relates to the subconscious mind. It relates to feelings and emotions. It also controls all the day-to-day workings of the body. It ensures that we breathe, for instance, and need to give no conscious thought to it.

In effect, the middle self thinks of something and the low self carries it out. The middle self is constantly feeding information into the low self. This is why it is important to think positive thoughts whenever possible. The low self makes no conscious decisions. If it is constantly filled with negative thoughts, it will produce negativity as a result. Likewise, if it is fed and nurtured with positive thoughts, it will function in a strong and positive manner. It responds well to repetition.

The low self also provides the middle self with information it receives from the senses. Pleasure and pain are two good examples.

The low self remembers everything. Everything that we have ever experienced or felt is stored inside the low self. These memories might be deeply repressed, but they are there all the same.

The low self is the feeling part of the body.

The High Self (Spiritual Self)

The high self is part of us, and separate from us, at the same time. It is the spiritual part of our makeup, and could be likened to a guardian angel that is always looking after us. It is your personal god. The Kahunas called it "the great parent." It is Mother, Father, and God in one. The high self will help us whenever we ask for it. However, it does not interfere with our free will.

The Kahunas addressed their prayers to their high selves, rather than to God. In fact, they did not understand the concept of a single all-powerful, omnipotent God. They agreed with the mystics that God is within each of us. Consequently, when they prayed, the Kahunas were actually praying to their high selves, the God within. This belief that they were gods enabled them to manifest anything they wanted.

The high self is the source of all inspiration, creativity, and pure selfless love. It is the source of hunches, premonitions and flashes of insight.

Each individual high self is connected with every other high self. It is also in contact with higher powers. This enables each of us to achieve anything we desire. All we need do is ask.

Aka

Our three selves are surrounded by an invisible substance or aura known as *aka.* This aka body changes shape whenever necessary to create connecting threads between our low, middle, and high selves. Each time one of our selves makes contact with another of our selves the bond becomes stronger, in time creating a strong braid-like connection that allows our three selves to work harmoniously together. We can achieve anything when our three selves are in perfect harmony in this way.

Everything is surrounded by aka. In other traditions it is known as the etheric or astral body. Even our thoughts are surrounded by aka.

We create aka connections with every person we meet, every place we visit, and every thought we make. These are fine strands of threads of aka substance. Thoughts and feelings can travel along these fine cords. This is why a mother often knows exactly how a child is feeling, no matter how far away they may be.

As we go through life, it is sometimes necessary to cut aka connections in order to progress. Our interests and goals change, and we sometimes have to let go of people and places that were previously important. However, we can never cut our aka connections to family. There are strong karmic links between family members, and if you cut them, you will have to repeat the lessons at a later date.

Mana

This is the final element of Huna. *Mana* is the vital life force that is the essence of life itself. It is the breath of life, divine spiritual energy. In different parts of the world mana is known as life force, ki, ch'i, or prana. We absorb mana every day from both air, and the food we eat.

The Kahunas used water to symbolize mana. When they wanted to accumulate mana for a particular purpose, they took deep breaths and visualized themselves as fountains filling up with water until they were overflowing.

Exercise and any other form of physical exertion encourages the low self to create more mana. This is how we get our second wind. We quickly use up the existing supply of mana, but then the low self immediately manufactures more to give us the energy we need. Consequently, we can create mana both by our thoughts (visualizing ourselves overflowing with water) and actions (physical activity).

We need mana to carry out our daily tasks. Any excess mana is used to help us achieve our desires and goals. Tension and stress use up a great deal of mana, leaving little for other purposes. Negativity also drains our supplies of mana. We are much more likely to suffer from illnesses and disease when our mana levels are low.

When we are full of mana we feel good about ourselves. We also have plenty of energy and vitality. We then have power to achieve our goals. The amount of mana we have is directly related to the amount of good fortune and success we have in life.

The Ten Elements

The different aspects of Huna can be divided into ten parts, or elements. The first of these is the physical body. Obviously, we cannot live in this world without our physical bodies.

We then have the three selves:

unihipili, or low self,

uhane, or middle self, and

aumakua, or high self.

The three selves are each surrounded by an aka body. The coarsest of these is the aka body surrounding the low self. It is sticky and attaches itself to anything it touches, creating fine threads of aka energy. The aka surrounding the middle self is finer and less dense than the aka surrounding the low self. The finest aka surrounds the high self. It is sometimes depicted as a halo.

Finally, the three selves each need different types of mana. The low self absorbs mana from food, water, and air. It is stored in the aka body and shared with the middle and high selves.

The middle self receives mana from the low self and transforms it in a way that doubles its power. It is called *mana-mana.* This mana-mana is used in the thinking processes and to send orders to the low self.

The high self requires a supercharged form of mana called *mana-loa.* We will learn how to create this shortly. Mana-loa enables the high self to manifest anything that is desired.

How to Achieve Your Goals

It is now time to learn how to manifest anything that you desire. All three selves are involved. You will understand why if you have ever tried to achieve something using the force of your will (middle self) alone, or simply desired (low self) something.

You can use the Huna ritual to achieve anything at all. However, there are two provisos.

1. You must use this ritual only for good purposes. The Law of Karma says that what you put out comes back. If you use the power of Huna for evil ends, you will ultimately have to pay the price.

2. You must know exactly what you want. Think about what you want, and why you want it. Most people want more money. Consequently, it is common for people to use this ritual to ask for, say, one-hundred-thousand dollars. However, money in itself is useless. You need to decide what you would do with the hundred thousand dollars, and ask for that. You might want the money to pay off a mortgage, buy a new car, go on an overseas trip, or to spend on luxuries. Ask for whatever it is that you want. If you want a new house, picture the house you desire in your mind. Picture the individual rooms, the garage, the garden, and everything else that you desire in your dream home. Of course, your desire does not have to be a material one. You might ask for a more peaceful home and family life, for instance. The most important factor is to know

exactly what you want, and to be able to express your desire clearly and concisely.

The Huna Prayer Ritual

Max Freedom Long called this ritual the "Ha Rite." *Ha* means "breath" in Hawaiian.

It is important that you conduct this ritual in private. It is also important that you do not discuss what you are doing with anyone else.

Choose a time and place where you will not be interrupted. You need to be as comfortable as possible. Make sure the room is warm, but not too hot. Wear loose-fitting clothing.

The process is simple and straightforward. You are going to send a request formulated by your middle self (conscious mind), from your low self (emotions) to your high self (guardian angel) through the aka cord. The request will be accompanied by an offering of mana to provide the power and energy for the desire to become manifest.

Step One: Filling your low self with mana

Stand with your feet about twelve to eighteen inches apart. Stretch. Think about the air surrounding you. Become aware that it is full of life-sustaining energy. Feel this energy surrounding you. It is mana.

Take a slow, deep breath. Breathe in through your nose and fill your lungs with as much air as possible. Feel the mana entering your body through your nose. Silently say, "I am filling my body with life-giving, life-sustaining mana."

Hold the breath for a few seconds, enjoying having your lungs full of positive mana energy. Exhale slowly.

Again become aware of the mana surrounding you. Take another deep breath, and repeat the process. Do this four or five times until you feel that your body is full of mana. (Some people prefer to repeat this stage three or four times before moving on to the next step. If you do this, allow a pause of thirty seconds before starting again.)

Step Two: Sending the mana to your high self

After taking four or five deep breaths sit down in an upright chair. Close your eyes. Picture yourself overflowing with mana. You might use the Kahuna image of seeing yourself overflowing with water. You might choose to see yourself looking vibrant and more full of energy than you've ever been before. It does not matter what picture you create, just as long as you are aware with every fiber of your being that your low self is full of an abundance of mana energy. This is the offering that you are going to make to your high self.

Once you have created a vivid picture in your mind, visualize a burst of energy coming from your solar plexus, up through your body and out of your head, forming a circle of energy immediately above you. You might see this as a gushing of water. Some people see it as a volcano of energy erupting. Again, it does not matter what you picture, just as long as you know, with every fiber of your being, that you are sending an abundance of mana to your high self. This mana is travelling along the aka cord that connects your low and high selves.

Step Three: Making your request (Part one)

Now that your high self is full of mana, you can make your request. You will have formulated this before starting the ritual. Have a clear picture of it in your mind. Superimpose this image on to the circle of energy above your head. If you are asking for a better-paying job, see yourself at work in the new position. If you want a new car, picture yourself out driving it. Visualize the exact model and color that you desire. If you are seeking better health, picture yourself completely healed. People "see" things in their minds in different ways. It makes no difference if you see it, feel it, sense it, or even hear it. The important thing is that you know, without a question of doubt, that whatever you have asked for will come to you.

Step Four: Making your request (Part two)

Visualize what you have asked for, for as long as possible. Now it is time to speak your request out loud. The exact words you use do not matter. However, you must say them in a strong, powerful, confident manner. You need to be totally certain that whatever it is you have asked for will come to you.

You might say: "I desire. . . . I want and desire it with every fiber of my being. I am asking you, my high self, to make this request a reality."

Step Five: Giving thanks

Pause for several seconds. Focus on your breathing to empty your mind of thoughts. When you feel ready, thank your high self for what it has done for you. Say thank you out loud, confident that your high self will bring to you whatever it is you have asked for: "Thank you, high self, for granting my request. I am grateful for all of your blessings upon me. Thank you."

If you like, you can say "father" or "mother" instead of "high self." Your high self is both male and female, and you can call it by either name, depending on your personal preference.

Step Six: Patience

The ritual is over once you have given thanks. You will feel excited, euphoric, and ready for anything. It feels much like a natural high. Some people experience tingling sensations. Others have a glowing sensation. Others have a sense of "knowing" that their request will be granted. Everyone is different, and consequently different people experience things in different ways. There is no right or wrong way.

After completing the ritual you can return to your daily life confident that your high self is working on your request and will bring it to you. You need total faith in your high self.

Repeat the ritual once or twice every day until your request is granted. It is important that you do not miss a single day.

How Long Will It Take?

Sometimes the request will be granted instantly. A friend of mine suffered constant pain in his knee. Doctors told him there was nothing they could do and he would have to learn to live with it. He performed the ritual, asking for the pain in his knee to go away. Shortly after giving thanks he noticed that the pain had completely disappeared and it has never come back.

Sometimes, though, it can take weeks or months, depending on what you have asked for. During this period you have to remain alert and aware of any opportunities that occur that can help you achieve your request. Your high self will not manifest your request out of nothing. It will, however, influence situations that will enable your request to be granted. It is up to you to seize the opportunities that occur.

Problem Solving

The process of making a request to your high self is a simple one. However, this does not mean it is easy. Many people become disillusioned when their request is not manifested. Fortunately, you can use your pendulum to ensure that your desires do become a reality.

You can use the pendulum at every stage of the process. Ask your pendulum about your request before starting the ritual. Find out if it would be good for you to have whatever it is you want at this stage in your life. Ask if your life will become better as a result of having it. Find out if other people would be adversely affected.

You may have emotional blockages that prevent the free flow of mana from your low self to your high self. Emotional problems are the biggest cause of failure in the whole process. You may have a variety of doubts and insecurities. There may be feelings of guilt. You may feel unworthy of receiving anything from your high self. You may have been deprived so often in your life that you feel uncomfortable when good things happen. You may have basic assumptions about work, money, and sex that you do not even realize you possess. These need to be changed before your request can reach your high self.

Remember that our emotions overrule logic every time. You may, for instance, consciously (middle self) desire more money, but if your emotions (low self) enjoy wallowing in poverty, and believe that you will never have any, the money will never come. To make it even more difficult, you may not realize that you have some deep-seated emotional problems. Fortunately, you can ask your pendulum questions about these. Here are questions that you can ask your low self:

Do I deserve success?

Am I worthy?

Am I a good person?

Am I a lovable person?

Do I have a fear of not being loved?

Do I enjoy helping others?

Am I sympathetic, tolerant, and understanding?

Do I express my feelings honestly?

Are there subconscious blockages that are holding me back?

Ask your low self as many questions as you can. You will find it remarkably informative and helpful. Once you find out what the blockages are, you can eliminate them by constantly feeding your low self with positive thoughts. Repeat affirmations that relate to love, health, harmony and success. At least once a day, repeat these affirmations while holding your pendulum. Rejoice whenever your pendulum reacts positively to these statements. It means that you have eliminated one of the factors that were blocking the aka cord between your low and high selves.

Your high self needs as much mana as possible. You can ask your pendulum if it has received enough mana to grant your request. Remember, though, that you can never give your high self too much mana. Any excess mana will be used for your benefit in some way.

Do not ask your pendulum if your request will be granted. This implies doubt in your mind. You need to remain absolutely, totally convinced that your desire will come into being.

Repeat the ritual at least once, and preferably twice, every day. Once you have eliminated anything that could be preventing success, nothing will prevent it from occurring.

Davina's Experience

Davina is a thirty-five-year-old accountant. She has been married twice. The first marriage ended in divorce and her second husband died tragically. Davina had been on her own for five years when she decided to use the Kahuna ritual to attract the right man to her. She was attracted to one of the partners in the firm at which she worked, but he had shown no obvious interest in her. She knew that she could only make requests that benefit everyone involved. Consequently, although she would have liked to ask her high self to send this man to her, she did not. Instead, she went through the entire ritual every day for two months. Finally, she realized that something was preventing her request from reaching her high self.

She asked her pendulum if she was ready for a new relationship. The answer was "yes." She asked if her desire for a permanent relationship was a good thing to ask for, and again received a positive response. She asked if she had finally managed to let go of the sadness and heartbreak of the past. Her pendulum responded positively.

She then began asking questions of her low self. Much to her surprise, she found that deep down she had a fear of rejection. Her father had left home when she was eight years old, her first marriage ended badly, and even her second husband had effectively left her when he died. She had a strong fear that any man she attracted into her life would sooner or later leave her. Her low self accepted and believed implicitly that this would happen. Consequently, every one of the requests her middle self sent to her low self about attracting a new partner were blocked. The request was never sent on to her high self.

Once Davina realized this, she began a program of filling her low self with positive thoughts about love and relationships. She wrote down these affirmations on cards and placed them everywhere. She stuck them to her refrigerator door and bathroom mirror, and put them in her handbag, on her dressing table, and inside the drawers of her desk at work. She repeated them constantly, and once a day said them while holding her pendulum. It took six weeks for her pendulum to give a single positive response.

After that, everything moved more quickly. Within a week, her pendulum was responding positively to all of the affirmations. She then resumed the Kahuna ritual, and three weeks later the man she was interested in at her office asked her out for dinner. She quickly discovered that he was not the man she thought he was, but it was a step in the right direction. After dating him a few times, another man showed interest and she went out with him for a couple of months. Five months later, and after dating several different men, she met Victor, a forty-four-year-old district attorney. She knew instantly that he was the man for her. They married several months later, and could not be happier.

If Davina had not consulted her pendulum, she would have become disillusioned with the Kahuna ritual, and would probably not now be happily married. The combination of the pendulum to discover and release emotional blockages and the Kahuna ritual worked perfectly for her.

Mana Charging

Mana contains amazing properties. It is the food that keeps our physical organism functioning, and maintains our three selves. However, it can also be used to charge anything with its extraordinary power.

Just recently, a friend asked me to suspend my pendulum over some muslin fabric that he had been given. I did not need the pendulum. As soon as I touched the fabric I instantly felt the incredible power it contained. It had been charged with mana energy and given to my friend to wrap around his frozen shoulder. Amazingly, his shoulder was restored to perfect health in a couple of days. He had spent weeks visiting a variety of healers, with no success, but the mana-filled muslin fabric cured him in forty-eight hours.

The good news is that it is possible to charge anything with mana energy. Your house, your bedroom, your workspace, a gift you intend to give to a friend, and even your pendulum can be charged with this amazing energy.

Stand with your feet twelve to eighteen inches apart, and take four deep breaths, holding each breath for a few seconds before exhaling.

Pause for thirty seconds, and then take another four breaths. Do this four times.

Sit in a straight-backed chair and send mana up the aka cord to your high self, in exactly the same way did with the prayer ritual. However, you are not asking your high self for anything this time. You are simply sending an offering of mana to your high self.

Now, take four more deep breaths. I stand before doing this, but it is not necessary. Remain seated if you feel more comfortable that way.

Feel this mana in your solar plexus. Pick up or touch the object that you want to infuse with mana. If the item is small, hold it in the palm of your right hand. Rest this hand on the palm of your left hand.

If the item is too large to hold, touch it with the palm of your right hand. If the object is not in your presence, visualize it in your mind.

Close your eyes and visualize the mana leaving your body through your right palm, and flowing into and around the object you wish to fill with mana.

Give thanks to your high self for the opportunity of using this mana energy to protect and charge the object.

Open your eyes.

The object is now charged with mana energy. Repeat this exercise, if possible, for four days to thoroughly imbue the object with this powerful energy.

You can easily prove the effectiveness of this if you have two objects that are identical. Charge one of them with mana energy. Ask a friend to determine which one is charged and which one is not. He or she should be able to do this without any difficulty. If your friend has problems determining which one is which, hand him or her your pendulum, and let it indicate the object that has been charged. Then ask your friend to mix the two objects while you are out of the room. When you return ask your friend to hand one of them to you. As soon as you touch the objects you will know which one is charged and which one is not.

You should charge your pendulum, and any other items you use in your magical work. This will provide protection and give the objects much more power.

chapter thirteen

Conclusion

YOU WILL FIND that your intuitive abilities will blossom once you start using your pendulum on a regular basis. There is no doubt in my mind that the pendulum effectively links our conscious and subconscious minds, allowing intuition to occur.

Naturally, you should use your common sense as well as the pendulum. With matters that are important to you, get as much information as you possibly can before acting. Your pendulum can be one of the methods you use to do this to gain insight into what is going on in your life.

Ignore the comments of skeptics. Nothing you do or say will change their minds. In the past I have tried to convert skeptics to my way of thinking, but it was always a waste of time and effort. It is also a waste of time trying to demonstrate how the pendulum works to them. Their negative energies will affect the demonstration and give them a chance to pour doubt and ridicule on you. People with closed minds resist anything new or different. In time, the quality of your work will speak for itself, and maybe, sometime down the track, a few of these skeptics will come back to you wanting to learn more about it.

The pendulum is a wonderful instrument you can use to help create magic in your life. However, the pendulum is nothing on its own, merely a weight attached to a thread. It needs you.

Practice, practice, practice. As you do, your success rate will steadily rise. It takes a year or more to thoroughly master the pendulum. Like anything else worthwhile, it takes determination and practice to be truly successful.

Use your pendulum wisely to create magic in your life, and to fulfill all of your dreams.

Notes

Introduction

1. Bruce Copen. *The Practical Pendulum.* Sussex, UK: Academic Publications, 1974, pp. 20–21.
2. Richard Webster. *Pendulum Power for the Psychic Entertainer.* Auckland, New Zealand: Brookfield Press, 1990, p. 9.
3. A. H. Bell. *Practical Dowsing: A Symposium.* London, UK: G. Bell and Sons Limited, 1965, pp. 14–15.
4. Michel-Eugène Chevreul. Quoted in *Pendulum Power for the Psychic Entertainer* by Richard Webster, p. 10.

5. Abbé Mermet (translated by Mark Clement). *Principles and Practice of Radiesthesia.* Longmead, UK, Element Books Limited, 1987. First published in French in 1935. First English translation published in 1959.

6. Raymond C. Willey. *Modern Dowsing.* Cottonwood, Ariz.: Esoteric Publications, 1975, p. 192.

Chapter Three

1. W. J. Finch. *The Pendulum and Possession.* Cottonwood, Ariz.: Esoteric Publications, 1971. Revised edition, 1975, p. 51.

Chapter Four

1. Richard Webster. *Dowsing for Beginners.* St. Paul, Minn.: Llewellyn Publications, 1996, p. 163.

2. Abbé Mermet (translated by Mark Clement). *Principles and Practice of Radiesthesia.* Longmead, UK: Element Books, 1987. Originally published in French in 1935, pp. 199–200.

3. W. H. Burgoyne. "Tracing the Lost." Article in *Practical Dowsing: A Symposium,* edited by A. H. Bell. London, UK: G. Bell and Sons Limited, 1965, p. 92.

4. Abbé Mermet. *Principles and Practice of Radiesthesia,* pp. 202–203.

5. Naomi Ozaniec. *Dowsing for Beginners.* London, UK: Hodder and Stoughton Limited, 1994, p. 103.

6. Abbé Mermet. *Principles and Practice of Radiesthesia,* pp. 207–208.
7. Henry de France. *The Elements of Dowsing.* (Translated by A. H. Bell.) London, UK: G. Bell and Sons Limited, 1948, pp. 66–67.
8. Richard Webster. *Dowsing for Beginners,* p. 45.

Chapter Five

1. Greg Nielsen and Joseph Polansky. *Pendulum Power.* Wellingborough, UK: The Aquarian Press, 1986, p. 13. (Originally published by Inner Traditions International Limited, New York, N.Y., 1977.)
2. Joseph Bulgatz. *Ponzi Schemes, Invaders from Mars, and More Extraordinary Popular Delusions.* New York, N.Y.: Harmony Books, 1992, p. 275.
3. Abbé Mermet (translated by Mark Clement). *Principles and Practice of Radiesthesia.* Longmead, UK: Element Books, 1959, pp. 172–173.
4. Arthur Bailey. *Dowsing for Health.* London, UK: Quantum Books, 1990.
5. In their book *The Healing Herbs of Edward Bach* (Hereford, UK: Bach Educational Programme, 1988), Julian and Martine Barnard say that suspending a pendulum over photographs of Bach flowers, or the plants that they come from, is an effective way of diagnosing a suitable remedy, p. 17.

6. Richard Webster. *Aura Reading for Beginners.* St. Paul, Minn.: Llewellyn Publications, 1998, pp. 29–38.

Chapter Six

1. Encyclopaedia Britannica, Micropaedia. Chicago, Ill.: Encyclopaedia Britannica, Inc., 15th edition, 1983, III, p. 616.
2. Richard Webster. *Practical Guide to Past-Life Memories.* St. Paul, Minn.: Llewellyn Publications, 2001.

Chapter Seven

1. Henri Mager. *Water Diviners and their Methods.* London, UK: G. Bell and Sons Limited, 1931, p. 31.
2. Richard Webster. *Aura Reading for Beginners,* pp. 29–38.
3. Richard Webster. *Aura Reading for Beginners* contains much more information on the meanings of the ground color, as well as the other colors in the aura.

Chapter Nine

1. Joe H. Slate. *Psychic Phenomena.* Jefferson: McFarland and Company, Inc., 1988, p. 45.

2. Richard Webster. *Dowsing for Beginners*, pp. 76–80.
3. Richard Webster. *Perma-Loss, the Permanent Weight Control Program.* Auckland, New Zealand: Prestige Marketing Limited, 1995.

Chapter Ten

1. Richard Webster. *Feng Shui for Beginners.* St. Paul, Minn.: Llewellyn Publications, 1997, pp. 4–6.
2. Bruce Copen. *Radiesthesia for Home and Garden.* Sussex, UK: Academic Publications, 1974, pp. 31–39.
3. Peter Tompkins and Christopher Bird. *The Secret Life of Plants.* New York, N.Y.: Harper and Row, Inc., 1973.
4. Ralph Whitlock. *Water Divining and Other Dowsing: A Practical Guide.* Newton Abbot, UK: David and Charles Publishers Limited, 1982, p. 43.
5. Sheila Ostrander and Lynn Schroeder. *Handbook of Psi Discoveries.* New York, N.Y.: Berkley Publishing Corporation, 1974, p. 42.

Chapter Twelve

1. Max Freedom Long. *Introduction to Huna.* Cottonwood, Ariz.: Esoteric Publications, 1975. Originally published in 1945.

2. The word "Kahuna" means "expert" or "authority." The Kahunas that interested Max Freedom Long were the ones involved in healing and sorcery. However, most Kahunas were not sorcerers. They were simply experts in whatever field they happened to be in. Consequently, Kahunas were master builders, fishermen, teachers, and priests. They became Kahunas after more than twenty years of training. Most came from the ruling class and were picked out as children, because of their natural ability and potential.
3. Max Freedom Long. *Recovering the Ancient Magic.* London, UK: Rider and Company, 1936.
4. Max Freedom Long. *Introduction to Huna,* p. 7.

Suggested Reading

Bach, Dr. Edward. *The Twelve Healers and Other Remedies.* Saffron Walden: The C. W. Daniel Company Limited, 1936.

Barnard, Julian and Martine. *The Healing Herbs of Edward Bach.* Hereford: Bach Educational Programme, 1988.

Barrett, Sir William and Besterman, Theodore. *The Divining Rod: An Experimental and Psychological Investigation.* New Hyde Park, University Books, Inc., 1968. Originally published in 1926.

Suggested Reading

Bell, A. H. (editor). *Practical Dowsing: A Symposium.* London: G. Bell and Sons Limited, 1965.

Berney, Charlotte. *Fundamentals of Hawaiian Mysticism.* Freedom: The Crossing Press, 2000.

Chancellor, J. A. *A Guide to the Bach Flower Remedies.* Saffron Walden: The C. W. Daniel Company Limited, 1971.

Copen, Bruce. *The Practical Pendulum.* Sussex: Academic Publications, 1974.

———. *Radiesthesia for Home and Garden.* Sussex: Academic Publications, 1974.

Cunningham, Scott. *Hawaiian Religion and Magic.* St. Paul: Llewellyn Publications, 1994.

Eason, Cassandra. *Pendulum Divination for Today's Woman.* London: Foulsham, 1994.

Finch, Bill. *The Pendulum and Possession.* Sedona: Esoteric Publications, 1971. Revised edition 1975.

De France, Henry. *The Elements of Dowsing* (translated by A. H. Bell). London: G. Bell and Sons Limited, 1977.

Graves, Tom. *The Diviner's Handbook.* Wellingborough: The Aquarian Press, 1986.

Howells, Harvey. *Dowsing for Everyone.* Brattleboro: The Stephen Greene Press, 1979.

Karges, Craig. *Ignite Your Intuition.* Deerfield Beach: Health Communications, Inc., 1999.

King, Serge. *Mastering Your Hidden Self: A Guide to the Huna Way.* Wheaton: Theosophical Publishing House, 1985.

Lethbridge, T. C. *The Power of the Pendulum.* Boston: Routledge and Kegan Paul plc, 1976

———. *The Essential T. C. Lethbridge* (Edited by Tom Graves and Janet Hoult). London: Routledge and Kegan Paul, 1980

Long, Max Freedom. *The Secret Science Behind Miracles.* Marina del Rey: DeVorss and Company, 1948.

———. *The Secret Science at Work.* Marina del Rey: DeVorss and Company, 1953.

———. *Growing into Light.* Marina del Rey: DeVorss and Company, 1955.

———. *The Huna Code in Religions.* Marina del Rey: DeVorss and Company, 1965.

Mermet, Abbé. *Principles and Practice of Radiesthesia.* Translated by Mark Clement. Longmead: Element Books, 1987.

Ozaniec, Naomi. *Dowsing for Beginners.* London: Hodder and Stoughton Limited, 1994.

Suggested Reading

Webster, Richard. *Dowsing for Beginners.* St. Paul: Llewellyn Publications, 1996.

———. *Feng Shui for Beginners.* St. Paul: Llewellyn Publications, 1997.

———. *Feng Shui in the Garden.* St. Paul: Llewellyn Publications, 1999.

Index

Index

Index

Index

Index